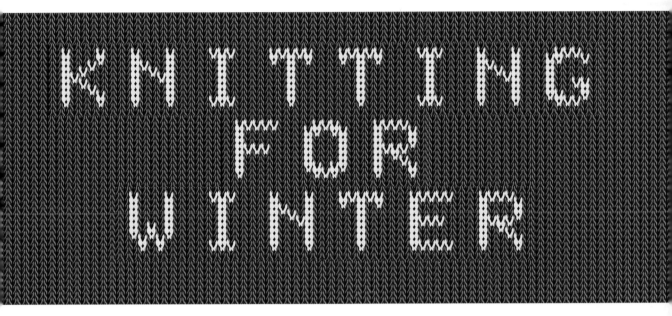

KNITTING FOR WINTER

Val Pierce

NEW HOLLAND

First published in 2015 by New Holland Publishers Pty Ltd
London • Sydney • Auckland

The Chandlery Unit 009 50 Westminster Bridge Road London SE1 7QY United Kingdom
1/66 Gibbes Street Chatswood NSW 2067 Australia
5/39 Woodside Ave Northcote, Auckland 0627 New Zealand

www.newhollandpublishers.com

ISBN: 9781742575650

Managing Director: Fiona Schultz
Publisher: Diane Ward
Project Editor: Holly Willsher
Cover Design: Lorena Susak
Internal Design: Peter Guo
Production Director: Olga Dementiev
Printer: Toppan Leefung Printing Limited

10 9 8 7 6 5 4 3 2 1

Keep up with New Holland Publishers on Facebook
www.facebook.com/NewHollandPublishers

Contents

Headband with Button, see project on page 48

Introduction

The art of knitting is gaining in popularity with each passing year and what was once a craft deemed somewhat old fashioned and boring has now taken centre stage. Knit and natter groups and clubs have sprung up all over the place, bringing together both young and old. Some folks want to learn, whilst others are willing to pass on their skills and some just like to spend quality time with like-minded people, sharing knitting stories and having fun.

With that in mind I have designed a collection of gorgeous, stylish, winter knits, some of which, even the less experienced knitter will be able to make. What better way to beat those chilly winter days than to snuggle up in a warm scarf or hat, especially when you have knitted it yourself! As with most of my books all the projects are star rated as to complexity, some are really simple quick makes whilst others need more time and experience to complete.

The projects range from chunky hats, scarves of many different types, mittens and gloves, to even a beautiful poncho and a Scandinavian style sweater for the guy in your life. No matter what your ability there is sure to be something that will catch your eye and entice you to begin knitting.

With the marvellous choice of yarns available these days it was quite the task to decide which to use for my designs. In this book I have opted to use some of the more exotic fibres since they give the finished designs a look and feel of pure luxury. These yarns are of course more expensive but it is nice to spoil yourself once in a while!

The projects are relatively small so the amount of yarn used for many of the designs is going to be minimal. I have given an alternative in each pattern so it is easy to substitute yarns for less expensive ones, provided you follow the stated tensions. There is also a section on the yarns used, their qualities and suggestions on how to care for your projects when washing them as extra care is going to be needed when using specialised yarns.

Whatever your preference I hope you will enjoy both knitting and wearing the designs in the book.

Have Fun and Happy Knitting!

Val Pierce

Hot Water Bottle Cover, see projects on pages 74 and 94

Techniques, Hints and Tips

TOOLS OF THE TRADE

When learning a new skill it is very important to have a good basic foundation of the techniques needed. In this section you will find hints and tips to help you achieve the best results possible.

Before you begin to work on your first project you are going to need the tools and equipment necessary. First and foremost you will need an assortment of good quality **knitting needles**. You can buy sets, neatly kept in a case or bag, which contain the sizes of needles most used in projects. Some people prefer the steel rigid needles, whilst others like the new bamboo and wooden needles which are more flexible, lighter in weight and "warmer" to use. It is of course personal preference as to which you purchase. Some patterns need **double pointed needles** to enable you to knit in the round, also **circular needles** come in very handy when knitting large amounts of stitches and also picking up and working front bands on garments. You may also like to add a **crochet hook** to your needle collection since these are invaluable when picking up dropped stitches.

It is also a good idea to buy a couple of **cable pins** and a **stitch holder** since these come in very useful and will be needed for quite a few of the designs in this book.

A **tape measure** is essential for measuring tension swatches and of course your projects as you make them. **Sharp scissors** and an assortment of **sewing needles** are also a must since you will need these when making up your projects.

Lastly it is always a good plan to have a knitting bag to keep your work clean and safe.

TECHNIQUES

This section describes the techniques required to teach you how to knit. You'll need time and patience to learn and perfect the different techniques, but with practice and determination you'll soon master the basics. It is inevitable that you will make mistakes, but that is all part of the learning process. You'll find in no time at all that you'll be knitting projects for your family, home and yourself!

Casting On

The first step in knitting is learning to cast on. This will form the first row of stitches and one edge of the finished project, this is normally the bottom edge. There are many ways of casting on. Here are the two methods that are mostly used.

TWO-NEEDLE METHOD

Knitting begins with a foundation row of loops cast on to a needle. The other needle is used to build a series of inter joining loops in rows, one after the other. Normally, you hold the needle with the stitches in your left hand and the needle to make the stitches in your right hand. (Left-handed people should work in reverse.)

1) Make a slip knot about 10 cm (4 in) from the yarn end and hold the needle in your left hand.

2) Insert the right-hand needle through the front loop and under the left-hand needle.

3) Pass the yarn under and over the point of the right-hand needle.

4) With the right-hand needle, pull the yarn through the slip knot to form a stitch.

5) Transfer the new stitch onto the left-hand needle, placing it beside the slip knot. Insert the right-hand needle through the front of the new stitch and under the left-hand needle.

6) Take the working yarn under and over the point of the right-hand needle to form the next new stitch. Continue in this way until you have the stated number of stitches.

Luxurious Legwarmers, see project on page 42

ONE-NEEDLE OR THUMB METHOD

1) This method gives a more elastic edge to the knitting. Leave a long length of yarn from the main ball to allow you to cast on the stated number of stitches. Wind the yarn twice around the thumb of your left hand.

2) Put the right-hand needle through the loop and pull through to form a slip knot.

3) Hold the needle in your right hand, wind the yarn clockwise around your left thumb and hold firm.

4) Insert the point of the needle through the loop, wind the yarn in your left hand around the back of the point of the needle and in between the needle and your thumb, and pull the tip of the needle under the thread, thus forming a stitch.

5) Slip the stitch onto the needle and close to the slip knot. The first stitch has been formed. Continue in this way until you have the stated number of stitches.

The Knit Stitch

Now you have mastered casting on, you can begin to form the first of two fundamental movements in knitting, *the knit stitch* and *the purl stitch*. Knit stitch forms a flat, vertical loop on the fabric face. Once you can work the knit stitch, you can begin to create a simple lined fabric known as garter stitch.

THE ENGLISH/AMERICAN METHOD

In this method, you use your right hand to pull yarn around the right needle. Winding the working yarn between your last two fingers controls the amount used for each stitch. Your left hand moves the knitting forward while your right hand makes the stitch, lifting the yarn, placing it over the needle and pulling it through the loop.

1) Holding the needle with the cast-on stitches in your left hand, wind the yarn around the little finger of your right hand, under the next two fingers and over the top of your forefinger.

2) Keeping the yarn at the back of the work, hold the second needle in your right hand and insert it into the front of the first stitch.

3) With your right forefinger, bring yarn forward, under and over the point of the right hand needle.

4) Pull yarn through the loop and push the resulting stitch towards the point of the left-hand needle so that you can slip it off onto your right needle.

THE CONTINENTAL METHOD

This method of knitting is often thought to be faster than holding the yarn in your right hand. Instead you use the forefinger of your left hand to keep the yarn under tension and to pull the yarn on to the right-hand needle. The fingers control the amount of yarn released. Raising your hand slightly will help to keep the yarn taught.

1) Holding the needle with the cast-on stitches in your right hand, wind yarn over your left forefinger, lay it across the palm of your hand and take up the slack between your last two fingers.

2) With the work in your left hand, extend your left forefinger, pulling the yarn behind the needle. By using your left thumb and middle finger, you will now push the first stitch towards the point then insert the right needle into the front of this stitch.

3) Twist right needle and pull the point under the working yarn to pull the loop on to the right needle.

4) It may help to hold the loop with your right forefinger while you pull it down through the stitch. Pull the new stitch on to the right-hand needle.

The Purl Stitch

The purl stitch is the other fundamental stitch used in knitting. When you use this stitch along with the knit stitch it will form stocking stitch. This will produce fabric which is flat and smooth on one side and has slightly raised lines on the other. Once you have learned and mastered these two techniques, the stitches will form the basis for a huge range of patterns. I will now explain the two most widely used methods of forming the purl stitch: English/American and Continental.

THE ENGLISH/AMERICAN METHOD

With this method the needle is put into the front of the stitch, then the yarn, which is held in the front, is wound over the back of the needle. Purl stitches sometimes tend to be a bit looser than knit ones so keeping your fingers close to the work will help to make the stitches more even.

1) Holding the needle with either the cast-on or knit stitches in your left hand, wind yarn around your little finger, under the next two fingers and over the forefinger of your right hand.

2) With the yarn at the front of the work, pick up the needle in your right hand and insert the point into the front of the first stitch on the left-hand needle.

3) With your right-hand forefinger, wind yarn over the point of the right needle and then under it.

4) Pull the loop on the right-hand needle through the stitch and push the new stitch towards the point of the left needle. You are now able to slip the stitch off your right-hand needle.

THE CONTINENTAL METHOD

When using this method, your left forefinger holds the working yarn tight while you pick up the new loop with your right needle. This movement is helped by twisting your left wrist forward to release the yarn and then by using your middle finger, you push the yarn towards the point of the needle.

1) Holding the needle with the stitches in your right hand, take the yarn over your left forefinger, lay across your palm and take up the slack between your last two fingers.

2) Holding the work in your left hand, push out your left forefinger slightly, pulling the working yarn in front of the needle. Using your left thumb and middle finger, push the first stitch towards the tip and insert the right needle into the front of the stitch. Hold the stitch with your right forefinger.

3) Twist your left wrist back and use the forefinger of your left hand to wind yarn around right needle.

4) Push down and back with the right-hand needle to pull the loop through the stitch, slip the new stitch on to the right needle. Straighten out your left forefinger to tighten the new stitch.

Casting Off

The technique of casting off is used to provide the finished edge of your work. It is also used when you need to shape pieces of work, or make buttonholes. Normally you would cast off on the right side of your work, however patterns will mostly tell you which side to do this. When using some patterns you will be told to cast off in the pattern that you are working in order to give a particular finish. Don't pull the stitches too tightly when casting off, this could result in a puckered edge or make it difficult to sew up the garment.

1) Work the first two stitches in pattern. ** With the yarn at the back of your work, insert the point of the needle through the first stitch. Lift the first stitch over the second stitch and then off the needle.

2) Work the next stitch in pattern ** now repeat the sequence set out between asterisks until the required number of stitches are cast off. You will be left with a single stitch at the end of the casting off, slip this off the needle and pull the end of yarn through it quite firmly to secure.

Increasing

When knitting a garment that requires shaping, you will need to add stitches, and this technique is called increasing. It is also necessary when you are creating certain stitch patterns, such as bobbles and lacy patterns. Where increases are made in garment shaping, they are normally worked in pairs so that the project widens equally on both sides of the work. Where increases are made in decorative patterns, they are combined with decreases so that the total number of stitches remains the same. There are quite a few methods of making increases in your knitting. The yarn-over method is visible and used in lacy patterns. The other methods are called invisible. In reality all increases are visible but some are more obvious than others.

THE BAR METHOD

This method produces a small horizontal stitch on the right side of the work and is most frequently used. You will knit into the front and back of a stitch to make two stitches. This type of increase is widely used on sleeve shaping or on garments where the resulting 'bump' will not matter if it shows.

1) Knit a stitch in the usual way but do not take it off the left-hand needle.

2) Insert the point of right-hand needle into the back of the same stitch and knit again.

3) Take the stitch from the needle in the usual way. The extra stitch formed by this method produces a small bump on the right side and is not very noticeable when it is worked on the edge of a garment.

MAKE ONE (ABBREVIATED AS M1)

Using this method you will pick up the horizontal strand of yarn that lies between two stitches and knit or purl into it to form a new stitch.

1) Insert the left-hand needle from front to back under the horizontal strand between the two stitches.

2) Knit or purl into the back of the strand on the left-hand needle.

3) Transfer the stitch back onto the right-hand needle. By twisting the stitch this prevents a gap from appearing in the work.

Decreasing

When you are knitting you may sometimes have to lose a few stitches in a row, such as when you shape an armhole or neckline. Casting off is the normal method used when you need to lose more than three stitches. If only one or two stitches have to be decreased you can use any of the methods described. Decreasing on garments are usually done in pairs that are symmetrical, V-neck shaping or raglan sleeve shaping are two prime examples. When the decrease is to the right of the centre, the stitch slants to the left; similarly, if the decrease is to the left of the centre, the stitch slants to the right. Right slants are made by knitting or purling two stitches together through the front of both loops; left slants are made by working through the back of both loops. Slip stitch decreases slant in only one direction, from right to left in the knit stitch and from left to right in the purl stitch.

KNITTING TWO STITCHES TOGETHER

RIGHT SLANT (K2TOG)

1) Insert the needle in the next two stitches through the front of both loops. Wind the yarn around the needle and pull it through.

2) Transfer the new stitch on to the right-hand needle.

LEFT SLANT (K2TOG TBL)

1) Insert the needle in the next two stitches through the back of both loops. Wind the yarn around the needle.

2) Pull the thread through and transfer the new stitch on to the right-hand needle.

THE SLIP STITCH DECREASE

This gives looser decrease than knitting two stitches together. When used on a knit row the decrease slants from right to left and is abbreviated as 'sl1, k1, psso'. A similar decrease can be made on a purl row, when the decrease slants from left to right. This will be abbreviated as follows, 'sl1, p1, psso'.

ON A KNIT ROW

1) Slip one stitch knitwise from the left-hand to the right-hand needle, then knit the next stitch.

2) Insert the left-hand needle into the front of the slipped stitch and pull it over the knitted one.

3) The right-to-left slant made by this decrease in a knit row is used on the right side of the centre of the work.

Cable Knitting

Using cables in your knitting can transform a plain and simple garment into something quite stunning and eye catching. They can be used on a single panel or they can be repeated on the garment to form an all-over pattern. The basis of all cable patterns is a very simple technique. Stitches are crossed over another group of stitches in the same row and some of the stitches making up the cable are either held at the back or the front of the knitting on a special cable needle, whilst the other stitches are knitted. The stitches on the cable needle are then knitted, forming a twist in the knitting. Cables can be worked over many different stitches and normally most patterns will state in their set of abbreviations how to work a particular cable.

RIGHT-HAND CABLE (WORKED OVER 6 STITCHES AS AN EXAMPLE)

When holding the stitches on a cable needle at the front of the work, this will always produce a right-over-left cable.

1) Slip the three stitches on to the cable needle and hold at the front of your work.

2) Knit the next three stitches on the main needle.

3) To complete, knit the three stitches that have been held on the cable needle.

LEFT-HAND CABLE (WORKED OVER 6 STITCHES AS AN EXAMPLE)

When holding the stitches on a cable needle at the back of your work, this will always produce a left-over-right cable.

1) Slip the first three stitches on to the cable needle and hold at the back of your work.

2) Knit the next three stitches on the main needle.

3) To complete, knit the three stitches held on the cable needle.

Picking Up Stitches

There are always neckbands, collars and possibly edgings on garments that will facilitate the need to pick up stitches from the edge of the knitted fabric. These stitches need to be picked up evenly all around the edge to give a neat, uniform finish to neckbands and collars. Where front bands need to be picked up, it is always advisable to measure and divide the stitches equally on the front and back neck so that the bands lie flat when knitted.

TO PICK UP A STITCH FROM AN EDGE

1) Hold your working yarn behind the completed piece and insert the knitting needle through it, between the rows and between the last two stitches of each row, from front to back.

2) Wind the yarn over the needle as if you were going to knit a stitch and then pull a loop of the yarn through to form a stitch. Continue in this way until the correct number of stitches has been formed.

Knitting with More than One Colour

There are many ways of enhancing your knitting by the use of colours. Nowadays there are a fantastic array of colours and textures available which will make your choice a very exciting one. One of the simplest ways to add colours to a garment is by making horizontal stripes, joining in the new shades of yarn at the beginnings of your rows. Combining different textures of yarns can also produce beautiful and stunning effects on your knitting, but care must be taken to make sure the yarns are of a similar weight or the tension produced may vary a great deal and as a result could spoil your garment. Other methods to incorporate colour can include block knitting, which entails using separate balls of yarn for each colour and then twisting the yarns together at the back of the work when changing colours to avoid making holes. Intarsia is another method widely used. It is more complex and complicated and you need to use a separate ball of yarn for each coloured stitch represented on a chart.

Working From a Chart

Coloured patterns and designs are often charted on graph paper and make it much easier for the knitter to follow. Each square on the chart represents a stitch and each horizontal line of squares represents rows of stitches. Charts can be either coloured or just black and white and they will always have a key at the side with different symbols depicting the different shades. You will read charts from bottom to top and normally from right to left. They are usually in stocking stitch and odd-numbered rows will be knit and even numbered rows will be purl, the first stitch of a chart being the bottom one on the right. Placing a straight edge of some kind, like a ruler or piece of card under each row will help you keep your place in the chart when working the design.

ADDING A NEW YARN WITHIN THE ROW

Follow this method when using the original yarn again in the same row. The yarn not in use has to be carried along the back of the work. When you have just a few stitches that need to be knitted in a different colour use stranding. If the distance between the stitches is more than around 5 or 6 stitches then weaving in is used. Failure to do this will leave long strands of yarn at the back of your work, which will spoil the fabric.

There are two methods of carrying yarns across a row when working with more than one colour. Both of which are explained below:

STRANDING

When using more than one colour in a row, the yarn, which is sometimes known as a float, is picked up and carried across the back of the work to make the new stitch. This yarn should be carried across the back of your work at the same tension as your knitting. If you pull it too tightly it will pucker the work, if it is left too loose your work will have holes or larger stitches where the different colours were changed. Much practice is needed to perfect this technique.

WEAVING

In this method, the yarn carried is carried alternately above and below each stitch made so that it is woven into the fabric as you go and is best worked using both hands. If knitting with many different colours, using small lengths of yarn wound around bobbins or cards will avoid any tangling whilst working. Weaving yarns will give a much thicker and less elastic fabric than stranding.

Lacy Stitches

Using yarn-over increases normally produces delicate and lacy designs. Fine weight yarns and small needles make lacy patterns ideal for shawls, shrugs or dressy scarves, and are perfect for pretty edgings to be used on garments or bags. Openwork patterns can be used in thicker fabrics too, these will give a more robust appearance to the garments. The two most widely used methods in openwork patterns are lace and eyelet. Lace is truly openwork, unlike eyelet which is solid work punctuated by small openings. Lace can be an all-over design or a panel, which is then combined with other stitches. Cashmere, alpaca, mohair, silks and cottons are amongst the many beautiful yarns that look stunning when knitted in lace patterns.

Yarn-Over in Stocking Stitch

1) To make a yarn-over in stocking stitch, bring the yarn forward to the front of the work, loop it over the right-hand needle, and then knit the next stitch.

2) The loop and new stitch are now on the right-hand needle.

3) Knit to the end of the row.

4) On the following row and with the rest of the stitches, purl the loop in the usual way.

Openings or holes are formed by the yarn-over increases; the same number of decreases will offset these so the number of stitches remain constant. Openwork needs stretching before it can be fully appreciated, therefore, if you are substituting a lace pattern for stocking stitch, cast on fewer stitches than the width requirement. Eyelets are another form of openwork. When made singly, eyelets can be used as buttonholes or for threading ribbon through and can also be used to form decorative motifs by placing them vertically or horizontally in combination with rows of plain knitting.

Tension

A major cause of headaches for so many people is "**Tension**". This small insignificant word that always appears on our knitting patterns, the little square that we all hate wasting precious knitting time making, when all we really want to do is get working on our new project to hand. What does tension mean? It is the resistance on the yarn as it passes through the fingers that are controlling it. Consistent, correct and exact tension is what every novice knitter is striving to achieve. **Tension** is **THE** most important thing with any garment you are going to make. This will determine the finished

Lacy Arm Warmer, see project on page 46

size of your garment, whether it fits you or is far too small or too big, it is so **IMPORTANT**. Taking that extra hour to knit one or maybe even two or three little swatches to get your tension right is so worthwhile. No cheating either, mark with pins, and keep measuring until you get it right. It doesn't matter what yarn you use as long as it is the same weight recommended. Don't be afraid to change needle sizes from the ones stated. All the hard work you are about to put into your project will be greatly rewarded when you finish your garment and it fits you perfectly.

Joining in New Yarns

Never join a new ball of yarn in the centre of a row, joining at the edge is so much better, this will give you a much nicer finish to your garment, trying to work in loose ends in the centre of a row will give a bulky spot or even maybe a small hole, which spoils the work. Unwind a good length of yarn when you are knitting and check that you are not likely to run out of yarn when finishing a row. If you do misjudge the amount then grit your teeth and pull back the row, you will be glad you did.

Rectifying Mistakes

Check back as you work, its much easier to pull back one or two rows to rectify a mistake than to finish a whole piece, make up the garment and then see a huge mistake looking you right in the eye!! If you do spot a mistake then stop working, unravel your work to the row above the problem, now pull back the row stitch for stitch until you reach the place where you need to rectify the problem. Lacy patterns are notoriously difficult to pull back so do take extra care if working those types of designs. If you drop a stitch then a crochet hook is invaluable in picking up the stitch and working back up the knitting row by row.

Measuring

When making a garment, measure as a rough guide for length, but always count the number of rows you knit to armholes on backs, fronts and sleeves before shaping. It is so much easier when making up a garment to match row for row. Measuring can sometimes leave you as much as four or five rows difference, then you would have to either ease the seam together or stretch it to fit or pull it back to correct the row difference. On most of the designs in this book you can easily add or subtract lengths to suit your own personal requirements, so headbands can be made smaller or larger, scarves can be shortened or lengthened, but do remember if you add extra length then you will need to buy extra yarn to accommodate that.

Finishing and Making Up

Making up your finished garment is equally important as tension. Many beautifully knitted garments have been ruined by poor making up. Most patterns will tell you the type of seaming they recommend for a particular design or yarn, but you can also read up in books, look on the internet and research if you are not sure. The many, many hours of work that you have put into this project deserves the very best finish. There are many different techniques to learn, the weight and texture and stitch pattern also can determine the way you should sew up the garment. Matching stripes and lacy patterns, making sure that seams are not puckered and ribbing sits flat and aligned is so important. Many of the projects in this book are knitted with bulky yarns made from pure wool or other natural fibres. Sewing these up needs extra attention, use a blunt ended wide eyed needle and use a short length of yarn at a time, constantly pulling long lengths of this type of yarn through fabric will cause it to wear thin and therefore break.

Not only do you want to feel proud of your masterpiece but you want to get admiring glances from others around you, and believe me you will.

Brioche Cable Beanie Hat page 30 and Stripy Mittens page 69

Scandinavian Sweater page 64

Detail from Fairisle Fingerless Gloves page 56

Knitting Terminology

When following a knitting pattern you will find that the instructions contain a special vocabulary, much of it is abbreviated. It can be a little confusing when you first begin to read patterns but you will soon get to learn the different meanings. I have listed below the most common terms and their meanings. When using the patterns in this book you will refer to them. On some patterns there are special abbreviations needed but these are listed on the instructions for that particular design.

ABBREVIATIONS.

K = knit

P = purl

St st = stocking stitch (USA Stockinet Stitch)

Cast Off. (USA Bind Off)

K2tog = knit 2 stitches together, thus decreasing a stitch

P2tog = purl 2 stitches together, thus decreasing a stitch

Tbl = through back of loop

Alt = alternate

Beg = beginning

Inc = increase

Dec = decrease

Rep = repeat

St = stitch

Sl = slip

Ssk = slip 1, knit1, pas slipped stitch over

Patt = pattern

Psso = pass slipped stitch over

Sl 1, K1, psso = slip 1 stitch, knit 1 stitch, pass the slipped stitch over the knitted one

Yfwd = yarn forward, thus making a stitch or a hole in lacy patterns

Yrn = yarn round needle

Yo = yarn over needle

RS = right side of work

WS = wrong side of work

Slouchy Beanie, see project on page 82

Poncho, see project on page 86

Luxury Yarns

A lot of the designs in this book have been made using luxury yarns or mixes of them. As most of the projects are quite small, the cost involved isn't too high. It is always nice to spoil yourself or a loved one with something special now and again and I am sure the lucky recipients will appreciate, not only the time spent making the project but also the knowledge that their gift is made using a special and luxuriously warm fibre. Having used these yarns then, you need to make sure you know how to care for them, so below I have written a little about each yarn, its properties and the best way to wash and dry it. You can of course substitute less expensive yarns for these designs and I have mentioned this on each pattern.

ALPACA FLEECE

Harvested from the Alpaca animals who are originally native to Peru, Chile and Bolivia, their fleece used to be reserved exclusively for the royal households and aristocracy during the Inca reign. Its fibre is soft, durable and luxurious and whilst similar to sheep's wool, it is much warmer, less prickly and since it contains no lanolin, it makes it a perfect choice for people who are allergic to wool. Pure alpaca yarns tend to be quite expensive so spinners now blend the yarn with wool or synthetics to give a warm yet more economical yarn to work with.

CASHMERE WOOL

Usually known as just **cashmere**, it is a fibre obtained from the Cashmere goat and other types of goat. Common usage defines the fibre as a wool but in fact it is a hair, and this is what gives it its unique characteristics as compared to sheep's wool. The word *cashmere* is an old spelling of Kasmir. Cashmere is fine in texture, strong, light, and soft. Garments made from it provide excellent warmth.

MOHAIR

Usually a silky fine yarn made from the hair of the Angora Goat, both durable and resilient, mohair is notable for its high lustre and sheen, which has helped give it the nickname the "Diamond Fiber" and it is often blended with other yarns. Mohair is warm in winter as it has great insulating properties, while remaining cool in summer due to its moisture wicking properties. It is durable, naturally elastic, flame resistant, crease resistant, and does not felt. It is considered to be a luxury fibre similar to cashmere, angora and silk and is usually more expensive than most wool that is spun from sheep.

ANGORA

Angora fibre refers to the downy coat produced by the Angora rabbit. While their names are similar, Angora fibre is distinct from mohair that comes from the Angora goat. Angora fibre is also distinct from Cashmere which comes from the Cashmere Goat. Angora is known for its softness, thin fibres, and what knitters refer to as a halo (fluffiness). It is also known for its silky texture. It is much warmer and lighter than wool due to the hollow core of the angora fibre. It also gives them their characteristic-floating feel. Yarns of 100% angora are typically used as accents. They have the most halo and warmth, but can felt very easily through abrasion and humidity and can be excessively warm in a finished garment. The fibre is normally blended with wool to give the yarn elasticity, as Angora fibre is not naturally elastic so this decreases the softness and halo somewhat as well as the price of the resulting yarn.

PURE WOOL

Years ago pure wool was quite difficult to care for, needed careful hand washing and drying flat. These days the wool has been produced and spun so that it is easy care and in some cases machine washable too. Funnily enough these days many of the pure wool yarns are used to "felt" accessories making them thick and matted, the very thing that years ago people wanted to avoid when washing their woollen garments. There are many types of wool, which are spun from different breeds of sheep and all have their own characteristic feel and texture to them. Rare breed fleece lends itself to natural colours and a more coarse feel, Aran weight yarns are sometimes oiled to give a water repellent finish and are perfect for the beautiful Aran patterned sweaters.

How to wash and care for your garments made in luxury yarns

Caring for luxury yarns does take a bit more time than usual but with a few simple rules to follow, your garments will give you plenty of wear. Firstly check the ball band on the yarn you used. Most spinners will give washing instructions for you to follow. If it states "hand wash only" then beware! Below I have given you some guidelines to follow that should make washing and drying your garment easy.

Always wash your woollens in tepid water and never expose them to direct heat. Heat is the enemy of wool and can lead to matting and shrinking. Wool is also very elastic and can easily be pulled out of shape with rough handling so wash things gently.

Use a mild detergent and swish your garment around in the water. You can soak it for around 5 or 10 minutes. Ball up the garment and gently squeeze the water out without wringing or stretching it. Use some fresh water and rinse until all the detergent is cleared. After squeezing out as much water as you can, lay the garment flat on a towel on a flat surface. Roll up the towel and garment together to remove moisture, squeezing and pressing as you do.

Dry your garment on a flat, moisture resistant surface and keep it away from sun and heat. You can lightly press or even steam a garment to remove any wrinkles if needed.

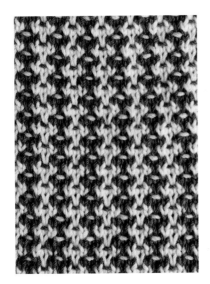

Detail from Hot Water Bottle Cover page 74

Detail from Shoulder Wrap page 84

Detail from Scandinavian Sweater page 64

Brioche Cables Beanie Hat

Clever chunky cables give a beautifully textured look and feel to this warm beanie hat. Although the pattern looks quite complicated, it is fairly easy to do. Practise the cable pattern before you commence working on the hat if you are a little apprehensive. The recommended yarn that I have used is a blend of cashmere and merino wool and is so soft and warm. There are gorgeous arrays of colours to choose from too.

MATERIALS

- 1 x 100 g (3 ½ oz) ball Rowan Pure Wool Worsted Aran, shade 104, Toffee*

- Knitting needles: Size 5.5 mm (UK 6, US 9)

* Alternate yarn: Use any aran-weight yarn with a similar tension to the one stated.

TENSION

20 sts x 25 rows measures measure 10 cm (4 in) square using 5.5 mm (UK 6, US 9) knitting needles.

ABBREVIATIONS

See Knitting Terminology (page 24).

Double Stitch = insert right hand needle into st below next st, K1, drop un-worked stitch above from left hand needle.

Hat

Using recommended needles, cast on 78 sts.

Row 1: * K2,P2,rep from * to last 2 sts, K2.

Row 2: * P2,K2, rep from * to last 2sts P2.

Repeat last 2 rows 3 times more.

Change to 12-row cable pattern and proceed as follows:

Cable Pattern

Rows 1, 3, 5, 7, 9: P3, *K7, P6, repeat from *, ending last repeat with P3.

All even rows: K3, *P1, work double stitch as follows: insert needles into st below next st, K1, drop unworked stitch above from left needle, (P1, double st) twice more, P1, K6*. Repeat from * to * ending last repeat with P3.

Row 11: P3, *work cable crossover on 7 sts as follows: slip 4 sts onto cable pin and hold at back of work, K3, then knit stitches from cable pin, P6*. Repeat from * to * ending last repeat with P3. **Rows 1–12** form the pattern. Repeat these 12 rows once more.

Shape Crown

Keeping pattern correct, proceed as follows:

Next row: P1, P2tog, *K7, P2tog, P2, P2tog, repeat from * ending last rep, P2tog P1 (66 sts).

Next row: K2, *pattern 7, K4, rep from * ending last rep, K2.

Next row: P2tog, *K7, (P2tog) twice, repeat from * ending last rep P2tog (54 sts).

Next row: K1, *pattern 7, P2, repeat from * ending last rep K1.

Next row: P1, *K7, P2tog, repeat from * ending last rep, P1 (49 sts).

Next row: *K3, K2tog, rep from * to last 4 sts, K4 (40 sts).

Next row: Knit.

Next row: *K2, K2tog, rep from * to end (30 sts).

Next row: Knit.

Next row: K2tog across row. 15 sts.
Break yarn, run through sts on needle, draw up and fasten off.

TO MAKE UP

Work in ends. Join seam on hat. Make a fluffy pom pom and sew to centre of hat, if liked.

Cabled Scarf

The stunning cables and twisted stitches make this a project for the more experienced knitter. Using a cashmere blend yarn will ensure this scarf is treasured both for its style and warmth.

MATERIALS

- 8 x 50 g (2 oz) balls of Debbie Bliss Cashmerino Aran, shade 062, Kingfisher*

- Knitting needles: size 4 mm (UK 8, US 6) and size 5.5 mm (UK 6, US 9)

- Cable pin

* Use any aran-weight yarn for the project, if you like, as long as you work to a similar tension.

TENSION

18 sts x 24 rows measures 10 cm (4 in) when measured over st st using 5.5 mm (UK 6, US 9) knitting needles.

MEASUREMENTS

180 x 20 cm (71 x 8 in)

ABBREVIATIONS

See Knitting Terminology (page 24).

SPECIAL ABBREVIATIONS

C2B: Slip next 2 sts onto a cable pin and leave at back of work, K2, then K2 from cable needle.

C2F: Slip next 2 sts onto a cable pin and leave at front of work, K2, then K2 from cable needle.

Tw2B: Knit into the back of the second st, do not slip the st off the needle, knit into front of first st and slip both sts off together.

Tw2F: Knit into the front of the second st, do not slip the st off the needle, knit the first st as usual and slip both sts off together.

Scarf

Using 4 mm (UK 8, US 6) knitting needles, cast on 44 sts.

Work in garter stitch (every row knit) for 12 rows.

Change to 5.5 mm (UK 6, US 9) knitting needles and commence pattern as follows:

Foundation row (WS): P1, K2, P2, K2, P10, K2, P2, K2, P2, K2, P10, K2, P2, K2, P1.

Row 1: K3, Tw2F, K1, (P1, K2, C2F, C2F, P1), K1, Tw2B, K1, P1, Tw2F, K1, (P1, C2B, C2B, K2, P1), K1,Tw2B, K3.

Rows 2, 4, 6 and 8: P1, K2, P2, K2, P10, K2, P2, K2, P2, K2, P10, K2, P2, K2, P1.

Row 3: K3, Tw2F, K1, (P1, K10, P1), K1, Tw2B, K2, Tw2F, K1, (P1, K10, P1) K1, Tw2B, K3.

Row 5: K3, Tw2F, K1, (P1, C2B, C2B, K2, P1), K1, Tw2B, K2, Tw2F, K1, (P1, K2, C2F, C2F, P1) K1, Tw2B, K3.

Row 7: K3, Tw2F, K1, (P1, K10, P1), K1, Tw2B, K2, Tw2F, K1, (P1, K10, P1) K1, Tw2B, K3.

These 8 rows are repeated to form the pattern.

Cont in patt until work measures 170 cm (67 in), ending on a WS row.

Change to 4 mm (UK 8, US 6) knitting needles and work 12 rows in garter stitch. Cast off.

Work in all ends neatly.

Cowl

Clever use of an elongated stitch gives an unusual detail to this pattern. Although it looks a little tricky, it is, in fact, very simple and can be attempted by the novice knitter. The yarn used is a blend of alpaca and lamb's wool and when knitted it gives a luxuriously warm and soft feel to the cowl. It is very easy to add extra length to the cowl, if you like, just remember to buy extra yarn.

MATERIALS

- 1 x 100 g (3 1/2 oz) ball Rowan Creative Focus Worsted, shade 00007, Lapis*

- Knitting needles: Size 5.5 mm (UK 5, US 9)

*Any aran-weight yarn can be substituted for this project as long as you work to a similar tension.

TENSION

15 sts x 18 rows measures 10 cm (4 in) over pattern using 5.5 mm (UK 5, US 9) knitting needles.

MEASUREMENTS

33 x 71 cm (13 x 28 in)

ABBREVIATIONS

See Knitting Terminology (page 24).

Cowl

Using recommended knitting needles, cast on 46 sts.

Proceed in pattern as follows:

Row 1 (RS): Knit.

Row 2: K4, purl to last 4 sts, K4.

Rows 3–6: Repeat rows 1 and 2 twice more.

Row 7: Knit.

Row 8: K4, *knit next st but wind yarn twice around needle before knitting instead of once, rep from * to last 4 sts, K4.

Row 9: Knit, but drop extra loop off previous row, thus creating an elongated stitch.

Row 10: Knit.

Repeat the last 10 rows until work measures 36 cm (28 in), or desired length, ending after a Row 9.

Cast off.

TO MAKE UP

Join the short ends of the cowl neatly together. Work in spare ends of yarn.

Flap-over Gloves

Knit these warm gloves to match the Beanie Hat design. The instructions provide patterns for men's and women's mittens. The flap-over mitten tops give warmth to your hands, while ensuring freedom of your fingers, if needed. A stylish Scandinavian-style pewter button on the mitten tops adds a little bit of extra detail. The yarn is pure soft extra fine merino wool and there is a vast array of colours to choose from.

Skill Level: Intermediate ××

MATERIALS

- 1 (2) x 50 g (2 oz) ball(s) Debbie Bliss Rialto DK, shade 23062*

- Knitting needles: Size 4 mm (UK 8, US 6) and size 3.75 mm (UK 9, US 5)

- 2 pewter-effect buttons

* You may substitute any DK weight yarn for the yarn used as long as you work to a similar tension.

TENSION

22 sts x 30 rows measure 10 cm (4 in) using 4 mm (UK 8, US 6) knitting needles.

MEASUREMENTS

To fit man's and woman's average hand

ABBREVIATIONS

See Knitting Terminology (page 24).

SPECIAL ABBREVIATION

M1: Make 1 stitch by picking up the strand that lies between the stitch you are knitting and the next stitch on the needle, and knit into the back of the stitch.

CUFF PATTERN

Row 1: Knit.

Row 2: Knit.

Row 3: P2, *K2, P2; rep from *.

Row 4: K2, *P2, K2; rep from *.

Flap-over Gloves

(Figures in square brackets are for men's gloves.)

RIGHT HAND

Using 3.75 mm (UK 9, US 5) knitting needles, cast on 42 (46) sts.

Work cuff pattern for 12 cm (5 in), [14 cm (5½ in)], ending on a second pattern row.

Next row: Purl, increasing 4 sts evenly across the row, 46 [50] sts.

Change to 4 mm (UK 8, US 6) knitting needles and st st, beg with a knit row, work 4 rows st st.

Shape thumb gusset as follows:

Row 1: K23 [25], m1, K3, m1. Knit to end.

Work 3 rows straight in st st.

Row 5: K23 [25], m1, K5, m1, knit to end.

Row 6 and every foll alt row: Purl.

Row 7: K23 [25], m1, K7, m1, knit to end.

Cont to inc in this way there are 58 [64] sts.

Next row: Purl.

Divide work for thumb
Next row: K38 [42], turn.

Next row: P15 [17], turn.

Work on these sts only for 2 [4] rows as follows:

Work 2 rows garter st. Cast off loosely.

With RS facing, rejoin yarn at the base of the thumb. Knit to end, 43 [47] sts.

Work 11 [13] rows without shaping, ending with a purl row.

Divide for Fingers
First Finger
Next row: K28 [30], turn.

Next row: Purl 13 [13] sts. Cast on 2 sts.

Next row: Working on these 15 [15] sts, K2 [4] rows st st.

Now work 2 rows garter st. Cast off loosely as before.

Second Finger
With RS facing, rejoin yarn, pick up and K2 sts from cast-on sts at base of first finger, K5 [6], turn.

Next row: P12 [14], turn and cast on 2 sts.

Next row: Working on these 14 [16] sts, K2 [4] rows st st.

Now work 2 rows garter st. Cast off loosely as before.

Third Finger
With RS facing, rejoin yarn, pick up and K2 sts from cast-on sts at base of second finger, K5 [6], turn.

Next row: P12 [14], turn and cast on 2 sts.

Next row: Working on these 14 [16] sts, knit 2 [4] rows st st.

Now work 2 rows garter st. Cast off loosely as before.

Fourth Finger
With RS facing, rejoin yarn and pick up and K2 sts from cast-on sts at base of third finger. K5 [5], turn.

Next row: Purl to end, 12 [12] sts.

Working on these sts only, work 2 [4] rows st st.

Work 2 rows garter st and cast off.

LEFT HAND

Using 3.75 mm (UK 9, US 5) knitting needles, cast on 42 [46] sts.

Work cuff pattern for 12cm/5in (14 cm/5 ½ in) ending on a second pattern row.

Next row: Purl, but inc 4 sts evenly across the row (46, 50) sts.

Change to 4 mm (UK 8, US 6) knitting needles.

Beg with a knit row, work 4 rows in st st.

Shape Thumb Gusset as follows:
Row 1: K20 [22], m1, K3, m1, knit to end.

Work 3 rows without shaping.

Row 5: K20 [22], m1, K5, m1, knit to end.

Row 6 and every following alternate row: Purl.

Row 7: K20 [22], m1, K7, m1, knit to end.

Cont to inc 2 sts as set in every foll alt row until there are 58 [64] sts.

Next row: Purl.

Divide for Thumb
Next row: K35 [39], turn.

Next row: Purl 13 (15, 17), turn.

Working on these 15 [17] sts only, work another 2 [4] rows st st.

Work 2 rows garter st, cast off loosely.

With RS facing, rejoin yarn at base of thumb and knit to end, 43 [47] sts.

Work 11 [13] rows without shaping.

Divide for Fingers
First Finger
Next row: K28 [30], turn.

Next row: P13 [13] sts. Cast on 2 sts.

Next row: Working on these 15 [15] sts, K2 [4] rows st st.

Now work 2 rows garter st, cast off loosely as before.

Second Finger
With RS facing, rejoin yarn, pick up and K2 sts from cast-on sts at base of first finger, K5, [6], turn.

Next row: P12 [14], turn and cast on 2 sts.

Next row: Working on these 14 [16] sts, knit 2 [4] rows st st.

Now work 2 rows garter st. Cast off loosely as before.

Third Finger
With RS facing, rejoin yarn, pick up and K2 sts from cast-on sts at base of second finger, K5 [6], turn.

Next row: P12 [14], turn and cast on 2 sts.

Next row: Working on these 14 [16] sts, knit 2 [4] rows st st.

Now work 2 rows garter st, cast off loosely as before.

Fourth Finger
With RS facing, rejoin yarn and pick up and K2 sts from cast-on sts at base of third finger, K5 [5], turn.

Next row: Purl to end, 12 [12] sts. Working on these sts only, work 2 [4] sts.

Work 2 rows garter st and cast off.

MITTEN TOPS

Make 2

With 4 mm (UK 8, US 6) knitting needles, cast on 44 (48) sts.

Work 6 rows in patt as follows:

Rows 1 and 2: Knit.

Rows 3 and 4: K2, P2 rib.

Rows 5 and 6: Knit, decreasing 1 st in centre of 6th row, 43 [47] sts.

Cont in st st for another 12 [14] rows.

Shape Top as follows:

Next row: K1, (sl 1, K1, psso, K16, (18), K2tog, K1) twice.

Next row and following alternate rows: Purl

Next row: K1, (sl 1, K1, psso, K14, [16], K2tog, K1) twice.

Cont in this way, dec 4 sts on every alternate row until there are 27.[27] sts left on the needle, ending on a purl row.

Cast off.

TO MAKE UP

Turn RS inside. Stitch up seams of fingers, working in ends of yarn as you go. Join main seam of gloves neatly. Turn fingers RS out and turn back the cuff. Stitch side seam of mitten tops. Turn RS out and then sew half of mitten top to the back of the glove, 6 rows below start of finger shaping. Make a small button loop by crocheting about 6 chains, depending on the size of the button you choose. If you cant crochet then make a loop of yarn the right size to fit over the button, attaching it to the mitten at both ends, now work buttonhole stitch all around the loop. Attach button loop to centre of mitt. Sew button to back of glove to correspond with the loop when the mitten top is folded back.

Luxurious Legwarmers

Two luxurious yarns are knitted together to give these pretty legwarmers extra thickness that will keep you warm and cosy on even the coldest winter day. An easy checkerboard pattern adds extra interest and is quite easy to work.

Skill Level: Intermediate ××

MATERIALS

- 2 x 100 g (3 1/2 oz) balls Stylecraft Alpaca DK (8-ply), shade Cream*

- 1 x 25 g (1 oz) ball Wendy Air Mohair, shade 2619, Bella

- Knitting needles: Size 5 mm (UK 6, US 8)

*Any DK (8-ply) weight yarn can be substituted. The mohair is a specialist lace weight yarn.

TENSION

18 sts x 20 rows measures 10 cm (4 in) using 5 mm (UK 6, US 8) knitting needles

MEASUREMENTS

35.5 cm (14 in) long

ABBREVIATIONS

See Knitting Terminology (page 24).

SPECIAL NOTE

Use 1 strand of DK (8-ply) and 1 strand of mohair together when knitting this project.

Legwarmers

Make 2

Using recommended knitting needles and 1 strand of each yarn, cast on 66 sts.

Row 1: * K2,P2, rep from * to last 2 sts,K2.

Row 2: * P2,K2, rep from * to last 2 sts P2.

Repeat last 2 rows for 10cm (4in) ending on a Row 2.

Now proceed with pattern as follows:

Row 1 (RS): *K3, P3*, rep from * to * to end.

Row 2 and all even rows: Knit all knit sts and purl all purl sts as they appear on this side of the work.

Row 3: *K1, yfwd, K2tog, P3*, rep from * to * to end.

Row 5: *P3, K3*, rep from * to * to end.

Row 7: *P3, K1, yfwd, K2tog*, rep from * to * to end

Row 8: As Row 2.

These 8 rows form the pattern and are repeated.

Continue in patt until work measures 34 cm (13 in). Change to K2, P2 rib, as shown at the

beginning, and work another 5 cm (2 in). Cast off.

TO MAKE UP

Sew in any ends. Sew side seam neatly, reversing seam for turnover at the top of the legwarmer.

You can add a tie if liked by making a twisted cord from the DK yarn and threading it through the top of the legwarmer.

Turban-Style Headband

Simple stitches and a two-row pattern are used to create this trendy turban style headband so that even a novice knitter can attempt this design. It is worked in a lovely soft cashmere blend yarn, which comes in an array of beautiful colours. I have chosen the colour Heather, but you are sure to find a shade to suit your taste.

Skill Level: Beginner ×

** You may substitute any aran-weight yarn for this design as long as you work to a similar tension.

MATERIALS

- 2 x 50 g (2 oz) balls Debbie Bliss Cashmerino Aran yarn in Heather
- Knitting needles: Size 5 mm (UK 6, US 8)

TENSION

18 sts x 24 rows measures 10 cm (4 in) when knitted using 5 mm (UK 6, US 8) knitting needles.

MEASUREMENTS

To fit average woman's head

ABBREVIATIONS

See Knitting Terminology (page 24).

SPECIAL ABBREVIATIONS

TW2F: Worked over the next 2 sts as follows. Knit into the front of the second stitch but do not take it off the needle, now knit the first stitch in the usual way, slip both stitches off the needle together.

Headband

Main Band

Using recommended knitting needles, cast on 29 sts.

Proceed in patt as follows:

Row 1: Knit.
Row 2: Purl.
Row 3: Knit.
Row 4: Knit.
Row 5: Purl.
Row 6: Knit.

These 6 rows form the ridge pattern and are repeated.

Continue in patt until work, when slightly stretched, measures 56 cm (22 in) ending with a Row 6. Cast off.

Centre Band

Using recommended needles, cast on 15 sts.

Row 1 (RS): K3, *TW2F, P1, rep to last 3 sts, K3.

Row 2: K3, purl to last 3 sts, K3.

These 2 rows form the pattern.

Work in pattern for 16 cm (6½ in) ending on a Row 2. Cast off.

TO MAKE UP

Work in ends neatly. Join short end of main headband. The join will sit at the centre front of the band. Take a needle and yarn and starting at the point where the band was joined, pleat the fabric together to draw in the band. Sew in place. Take the centre band and place around the pleated area. Sew the short ends of the band together and then secure it to the headband with a few stitches.

Lacy Arm Warmers

A beautifully soft alpaca wool mix yarn is used for these pretty arm warmers. The pattern is not complicated and consists of a 6-row repeat. I chose new season colour plum, but there are some gorgeous mixed shades offered in this yarn. You can easily convert the pattern to wrist warmers by working a shorter length.

Skill Level: Intermediate ××

MATERIALS

- 1 x 100 g (3 1/2 oz) ball of Stylecraft Alpaca Tweed DK (8-ply), shade 1665, Plum
- Knitting needles: Size 4 mm (UK 8, US 6)

TENSION

23 sts x 29 rows measures 10 cm (4 in) using 4 mm (UK 8, US 6) knitting needles

MEASUREMENTS

Length 30 cm (12 in); diameter 25 cm (10 in)

ABBREVIATIONS

See Knitting Terminology (page 24).

Arm Warmers

Make 2

Using recommended needles, cast on 49 sts.

Work 4 rows in garter st.

Begin pattern as follows:

Row 1: K1, *yfwd, K2, sl 1, K2tog, psso, K2, yfwd, K1, rep from * to end.

Rows 2 and 4: Purl.

Row 3: K2, *yfwd, K1, sl 1, K2tog, psso, K1, yfwd, K3, rep from * to last 7 sts, yfwd, K1, sl 1, K2tog, psso, K1, yfwd, K2.

Row 5: K3, *yfwd, sl 1, K2tog, psso, yfwd, K5, rep from * to last 6 sts, yfwd, sl 1, K2tog, psso, yfwd, K3.

Row 6: Purl.

These 6 rows form pattern and are repeated (this is the top of the arm warmer).

Work another 11 repeats of pattern (you can add to, or subtract from, the length, if you like, by working more or less pattern repeats).

Change to garter st and work 6 rows. Cast off.

TO MAKE UP

Fold piece in half lengthways. Join side seam starting from top for 5 cm (2 in). Leave a gap for thumbhole of 6 cm (2 1/4 in) long. Join rest of seam matching patterns. Make the other arm warmer in the same way.

Headband with Button

A lovely soft cashmere blend of yarn is used to create this pretty headband. The textured pattern is created by working an easy 4-row pattern of twisted stitched. Complete the look of the headband by adding a decorative matching button.

MATERIALS

- 2 x 50 g (2 oz) balls Debbie Bliss Cashmerino Aran, shade 202, Silver

- 1 large matching button

- Knitting needles: Size 5 mm (UK 6 US 8)

TENSION

18 sts x 24 rows measures 10 cm (4 in) using 5 mm (UK 6, US 8) knitting needles.

MEASUREMENTS

To fit average size woman's head.

ABBREVIATIONS

See Knitting Terminology (page 24).

SPECIAL ABBREVIATIONS

TW2B: Worked over the next 2 sts as follows: Knit into back of second st, do not slip stitch off needle. Knit first stitch in the usual way and slip both stitches off the needle together.

TW2F: Worked over the next 2 sts as follows: Knit into front of second st, do not slip stitch off needle, knit first stitch in the usual way and slip both stitches off the needle together

Headband

Using recommended knitting needles, cast on 28 sts.

Begin pattern as follows:

Row 1 (RS): K3, P2, *TW2B, P2, rep from * to last 3 sts, K3.

Row 2: K5, *P2, K2, rep from * to last 5 sts, K5.

Row 3: K3, P2, *TW2F, P2, rep from * to last 3 sts, K3.

Row 4: K5, *P2, K2 , rep from * to last 5 sts, K5.

These 4 rows form the pattern and are repeated throughout.

Continue in pattern until work measures 52 cm (20½ in).

Keeping continuity of the pattern as you decrease, shape end as follows:

Next row: K3, P2tog, pattern to last 5 sts, P2tog, K3.

Next row: K3, pattern to last 3 sts, K3.

Cont to dec 1 st at each end inside the garter stitch border until 8 sts remain.

Next row: K3, K2tog, K3.

Next row: K7.

Next row: K2, sl 1, K2tog, psso, K2.

Next row: K5.

Next row: K1, sl1, k2tog, psso, K1.

Next row: K3tog and fasten off.

TO MAKE UP

Work in ends. Overlap headband and join at the point where shaping began. Sew button to finishing point of work and catch down to headband.

Slipper Socks with Bobble Ties

Pure wool makes these gorgeous slipper socks a perfect gift for anyone. Add a tie and pom poms for an even more attractive effect. The patterning is quite complex and needs concentration but when finished it gives a lovely chunky texture to the fabric.

TIP

Add some puff paint dots or squiggles to the foot of the sock if you liked to create a less slippery surface.

MATERIALS

- 2 x 100 g (3 1/2 oz) balls Stylecraft Alpaca Tweed DK (8-ply) yarn, shade 1661, Sage
- Knitting needles: Size 4.5 mm (UK 7, US 7)

SIZE

To fit woman's average foot length.

SPECIAL ABBREVIATIONS

TW2F: Knit into the front of the second stitch, do not slip off needle, now knit the first stitch in the usual way, slip both stitches off at the same time.

Slipper socks

Cast on 54 sts using recommended knitting needles.

Row 1: K2, *P2, K2*, repeat from * to * across the row.

Row 2: P2, *K2, P2*, repeat from * to * across the row.

Repeat last 2 rows 6 more times.

Begin pattern

Row 1 (WS): P4, K2, P2, K2, P4*, rep from * to end.

Row 2: K4, *P2, TW2F, P2, K4*, rep from * to end.

Repeat last 2 rows once more.

Row 5: K1, P2, *K2, P4, K2, P2*, rep from * to last st, K1.

Row 6: P1, TW2F, *P2, K4, P2, TW2F*, rep from * to last st, P1.

Rep last 2 rows once more.

These 8 rows form pattern. Continue until work measures 25 cm (10 in) ending on a Row 1.

Divide for Heel

Row 1 (WS): Sl 1, P13.

Row 2: Knit.

Repeat these 2 rows 6 times more, then work Row 1 once more.

Turn Heel

Row 1 (RS): K3, skpso, K1, turn.

Row 2: Sl1, P4, turn.

Row 3: K4, skpso, K1, turn.

Row 4: Sl 1, P5, turn.

Row 5: K5, skpso, K1, turn.

Row 6: Sl 1, P7.

Row 7: K6, skpso, K1, turn.

Row 8: Sl1, P7, turn.

Row 9: K7, skpso, K1.

Row 10: Sl 1, P8.

Row 11: K9, pick up and K8 sts down side of heel, P2, TW2F, P2, K4, P2, TW2F, P2, K4, P2, TW2F, P2, K14.

Row 12: P14, turn.

Work on these 14 sts as follows:

Row 1: K14.

Row 2: Sl 1, P13.

Repeat these 2 rows another 5 times then Row 1 again.

Second Half of Heel

Turn heel.

Row 1 (WS): P3, P2tog, P1, turn.

Row 2: Sl 1, K4, turn.

Row 3: P4, P2tog, P1, turn.

Row 4: Sl 1, K5, turn.

Row 5: P5, P2tog, P1, turn.

Row 6: Sl 1, K7, turn.

Row 7: P7, p2tog, P1, turn.

Row 8: Sl 1, K8, turn.

Next row: P9, pick up and purl 8 sts down side of heel, K2, P2, K2, P4, K2, P2, K2, P4, K2, K2, P2, purl across last 17 sts.

Keeping continuity of the centre pattern with st st panels on each side, shape the gusset.

Gusset

Row 1 (RS): K15, K2togtbl, patt K26, K2tog, K15.

Row 2: P16, patt 26, P16.

Row 3: K14, K2togtbl, patt K26, K2tog, K14.

Row 4: P15, patt 26, P15.

Row 5: K13, K2togtbl, patt K26, K2tog, K13.

Row 6: P14, patt 26, P14

Row 7: K12. K2tog, K26, ssk, K9.

Row 8: P13, patt 26, P13.

Row 9: K11, K2tog, K26, ssk, K11.

Row 10: P12, patt 26, P12.

Row 11: K10, K2tog tbl, patt 26, K2tog, K10.

Row 12: P11, patt 26, P11 (48 sts).

Foot shaping complete.

Continue across all sts, working 11 sts each end in st st, and the centre 26 in pattern until work measures 12.5 cm (5 in) or desired foot length.

SHAPE TOE

Continue in st st only.

Row 1: K9, K2tog, K2, ssk, K18, K2tog, K2, ssk, K9.

Row 2 and all even rows: Purl.

Row 3: K8, K2tog, K2, ssk, K16, K2tog, K2, ssk, K8.

Cont decreasing 4 sts on every other row in this way until 24 sts remain. Cast off..

TO MAKE UP

Sew in all ends neatly. Join seams using a very flat seam. Make two twisted cords each 65 cm (25 1/2 in) long. Make two pom poms for each cord. Using a big crochet hook, thread the cords through the top of the fabric of the sock just below the ribbing. Make sure you finish at opposite sides on each sock. Attach the pom poms to the ends of the cords.

Fairisle Fingerless Gloves

A band of easy Fairisle pattern adds extra interest to these warm fingerless gloves. The yarn used is pure Yorkshire wool, which has a soft roving feel. The colours available are earthy and subtle and it is very attractive to work with.

Skill Level: Intermediate ××

MATERIALS

- Wendy Ramsdale DK (8-ply) (112 m /122 yd per 50 g/2 oz ball)
- Richmond: A (Apple)
- Malham: B (Cream)
- Thirsk: C (Burnt Orange)
- Knitting needles: Size 3.75 mm (UK 9, US 5) and size 4 mm (UK 8, US 6)

** Any DK (8-ply) weight yarn can be substituted for this project as long as the tension is similar.

MEASUREMENTS

To fit woman's average hand.

TENSION

20 st x 28 rows measures 10 cm (4 in) using 4 mm (UK 8, US 6) knitting needles.

RIGHT HAND

Using 3.75 mm (UK 9, US 5) knitting needles and C, cast on 42 sts.

Work in K2, P2 rib for 2 rows. Break off C and join in B.

Continue in rib for another 20 rows, increasing 4 sts evenly across last row (46 sts).

Change to 4 mm (UK 8, US 6) knitting needles and beginning with a knit row work 4 rows sts.

Shape Thumb Gusset:

Row 1: K23, m1, K3, m1, knit to end.

Work 3 rows st st.

Row 5: K23, m1, K5, m1, knit to end.

Row 6 and every following alternate row: Purl.

Row 7: K23, m1, K7, m1, knit to end.

Continue to increase in this way until you have 58 sts.

Next row: Purl.

Divide work for thumb:

Next row: K38, turn.

Next row: P15, turn.

Work on these stitches only for 4 rows. Break B and join in C.

Now work 2 rows garter stitch. Cast off loosely.

With RS facing, rejoin yarn B at the base of the thumb, knit to end (43 sts).

Beg with a purl row, work 3 rows st st.

Join in A and C and work 9 rows pattern band from chart. Break A and C and continue in B.

Next row: Purl.

Divide for Fingers:

First Finger
Next row: K28, turn.

Next row: P13. Cast on 2 sts.

Next row: Working on these 15 sts, knit 4 rows st st. Break yarn B and join in yarn C

Work 2 rows garter stitch. Cast off loosely.

Second Finger
With RS facing , rejoin yarn B, and pick up and knit 2 sts from cast-on sts at base of first finger, K5, turn.

Next row: P12, turn and cast on 2 sts.

Next row: Working on these 14 sts, knit 4 rows st st. Break off yarn B and join in yarn C.

Work 2 rows garter stitch. Cast off loosely.

Third Finger
With RS facing, rejoin yarn B, and pick up and knit 2 sts from cast-on sts at base of second finger, K5, turn.

Next row: P12, turn and cast on 2 sts.

Next row: Working on these 14 sts, knit 4 rows st st. Break off yarn B and join in yarn C.

Work 2 rows garter stitch. Cast off loosely.

Fourth Finger
With RS facing, rejoin yarn B and pick up and knit 2 sts from cast-on sts at base of third finger, K5, turn.

Next row: Purl to end (12 sts).

Working on these sts only, work 4 rows st st. Break off yarn B and join in yarn C.

Work 2 rows garter stitch and cast off.

LEFT HAND

Using 3.75 mm (UK 9, US 5) knitting needles and yarn C, cast on 42 sts.

Work in K2, P2 rib for 2 rows. Break off yarn C and join in yarn B.

Continue in rib for another 20 rows, increasing 4 sts evenly across last row (46 sts).

Change to 4 mm (UK 8, US 6) knitting needles and begin with a knit row work 4 rows st st.

Shape Thumb Gusset as follows:

Row 1: K20, m1, K3, M1, knit to end.

Work 3 rows without shaping.

Row 5: K20, m1, K5, m1, knit to end.

Row 6 and every following alternate row: Purl.

Row 7: K20, m1, K7, m1, knit to end.

Cont to inc 2 sts as set in every following alternate row until there are 58 sts.

Next row: Purl.

Divide for Thumb

Next row: K35, turn.

Next row: P15, turn.

Working on these 15 sts only, work another 4 rows st st. Break off yarn B and join in yarn C.

Work 2 rows garter st. Cast off loosely.

With RS facing, rejoin yarn B at the base of the thumb and knit to end (43 sts).

Beg with a purl row, work 3 rows st st.

Join in yarns A and C and work 9 rows patterning from chart below. Break A and C.

Continue in B and purl 1 row.

Divide for Fingers

First Finger
Next row: K28, turn.

Next row: P13 sts. Cast on 2 sts.

Next row: Working on these 15 sts, knit 4 rows st st. Break off yarn B and join in yarn C.

Work 2 rows garter stitch. Cast off loosely.

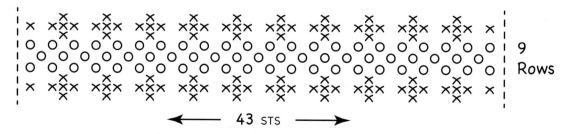

43 STS

KEY for Yarn shades: x = Apple Green (A)
o = Burnt Orange (C)

9 Rows

Second Finger

With RS facing, rejoin yarn B, and pick up and K2 sts from cast-on sts at base of first finger, K5, turn.

Next row: P12, turn and cast on 2 sts.

Next row: Working on these 14 sts, knit 4 rows st st. Break off yarn B and join in yarn C.

Now work 2 rows garter stitch. Cast off loosely.

Third Finger

With RS facing, rejoin yarn B. Pick up and knit 2 sts from cast-on sts at base of second finger, K5, turn.

Next row: P12, turn and cast on 2 sts.

Next row: Working on these 14 sts, knit 4 rows st st. Break off yarn B and join in yarn C.

Now work 2 rows garter stitch. Cast off loosely as before.

Fourth Finger

With RS facing, rejoin yarn B and pick up and K2 sts from cast-on sts at base of third finger, K5, turn.

Next row: Purl to end (12 sts).

Working on these 12 sts only, work 4 rows st st. Break off yarn B join in yarn C.

Work 2 rows garter stitch and cast off.

TO MAKE UP

Turn RS inside. Now begin to stitch up seams of fingers, working in ends of yarn as you go. Join main seam of gloves neatly. Turn RS out and turn back cuff, if liked.

Hand Warmers

Keep your hands warm while leaving your fingers free with these pretty hand warmers. The yarn used is pure wool and so soft to touch. It comes in a range of lovely shades so there will be something to suit all tastes. Knitted on big needles and using a simple slipped stitch pattern, you can make them in just a couple of evenings.

MATERIALS

- 30 g (1 oz) of each of the following Hayfield DK with Wool DK (8-ply)*** (300 m/328 yd per 100 g/4oz ball)

- Gurnsey, shade 90 (A)

- Camelia, shade 108 (B)

- Sand, shade 91 (C)

- Knitting needles: Size 5 mm (UK 6, US 8)

***You can substitute any DK (*-ply) weight yarn as long as it is a similar tension.

MEASUREMENTS

To fit woman's average hand.

Length: 17 cm (6½ in); width around palm: 21 cm (8¼ in)

TENSION

20 sts x 25 rows measured over 10 cm (4 in) when knitted on recommended knitting needles

ABBREVIATIONS

See Knitting Terminology (page 24).

SPECIAL ABBREVIATIONS

Tbl: Through back of loop.

Hand Warmers

Make 2

Using recommended knitting needles and yarn B, cast on 36 sts.

Row 1: *K2tbl, P2*, rep from * to * to end.

Repeat last row 15 times more. Break off yarn B and join in yarn C

Work 4 rows st st. Join in yarn A.

Next row: K2, *sl1, K3*, rep to last 2 sts, sl1, K1.

Next row: P1, sl1, *P3, sl 1, rep to last 2 sts, P2.

Work 4 rows st st. Join in yarn C.

Next row: K4, *sl1, K3*, rep to end.

Next row: *P3, sl1*, rep to last 4 sts, P4.

Work 4 rows st st. Join in yarn A.

Next row: K2, *sl 1, K3*, rep to last 2 sts, sl 1, K1.

Next row: *P1, sl 1, *rep to last 2 sts, P2.

Work 4 rows st st. Join in yarn C.

Work 4 rows in K2tbl, P2 rib. Join in yarn A.

Work 4 rows K2tbl, P2 rib.

Join in yarn B and work 2 rows in K2tbl, P2 rib.

Cast off in rib.

TO MAKE UP

Sew seams on pieces, matching stripes and colours as you work. Remember to leave a small opening approximately 4 cm (1 3/4 in) below the top of the wrist warmer for the thumb hole. Work in all yarn ends neatly on the WS of the work.

Simple House Slippers

Chunky yarn and large needles are used to make these cozy house slippers. They are knitted in simple garter stitch and can be made in just a couple of evenings, even by a novice. They are intended for use on carpeted areas. If you want to use them on hard wood or tiled floors then add some puff paint to the soles to give grip.

MATERIALS

- 1 x 200 g (7 oz) ball James C Brett Marble Chunky yarn, shade 33, Light Green Mix.*
- Knitting needles: Double ended needles size 4.0mm (UK 8, US 6)
- 1 x 50grm ball DK Sirdar Country Style in shade Garnet 418

*Any chunky-weight yarn (312 m/341 yd to 200 g/7 oz ball) may be substituted for this project as long as you check the tension.

TENSION

14 sts x 20 rows measure 10 cm (4 in) when knitted using 6 mm (UK 4, US 10) knitting needles.

MEASUREMENTS

To fit woman's average foot size.

ABBREVIATIONS

See Knitting Terminology (page 24).

Slippers

Make 2

Using recommended knitting needles, cast on 37 sts.

Work in garter st (every row knit) for 13 cm (5 in)

Next row: K2tog at each end of the row.

Rep last row 3 more times (29 sts) Place marker here.

Cont on these sts until work measures 23 cm (9 in).

Next row: K2tog across row to last st, K1 (15 sts).

Work 3 rows in garter st.

Next row: *K2tog, K3, rep from * twice more (13 sts).

Next row: Knit.

Next row: (K2tog) 6 times, K1.

Break yarn and run through sts on needle, draw up and fasten off. (This is the toe end.)

TO MAKE UP

Fold the slipper in half lengthways, sew up the heel neatly. Now sew up the top of the slipper from toe to marked place. Fold over the rim of the slipper onto the right side of the work and catch down all the way around. Using double ended needles cast on 6 sts and work an i cord long enough to fit around the top cuff of the slipper plus 10cm (8in) extra to allow for the design on the front. Mark centre of i cord, sew the centre to the centre back of the slipper, now stitch around each side of the cuff, fold the ends over to form a decorative loop on the front of the slipper. Finish other slipper in the same way.

Scandinavian Sweater

Scandinavian patterning and a pure wool chunky yarn are used for this warm sweater. Time and patience will be required when working the design but your efforts will be well rewarded when your project is complete. The stranding method is used when working the patterning so do take care not to pull the yarn too tightly as you work.

MATERIALS

- 11 x 50 g (2 oz) balls Bergere de France Magic+ Chunky in Calot, shade 290 401*

- 2 x 50 g (2 oz) balls Bergere de France Magic+ Chunky in Avalanche, shade 207 391

- 2 x 50 g (2 oz) balls Bergere de France Magic+ Chunky in Adriatique, shade 218 171

- Knitting needles: Size 5.5 mm (UK 5, US 9) and 6 mm (UK 4, US 10)

*Any chunky-weight yarn (80 m/87 yd per 50 g /2 oz ball) with a similar tension can be used for this garment.

NOTE: All charts are read from right to left beginning Row 1 with Knit.

TENSION

16 sts x 20 rows = 10 cm (4 in) worked over st st using 6 mm (UK 4, US 10) knitting needles.

MEASUREMENTS

To fit chest: 102–107cm (40–42 in); Length: 74 cm (29 in); Sleeve seam: 54 cm (21 in)

ABBREVIATIONS

See Knitting Terminology (page 24).

SPECIAL ABBREVIATIONS

Tbl: Through back of loop

Twisted Rib: k2tbl, P2

Sweater

Back

Using Adriatique, and size 5.5 mm (UK 5, US 9) knitting needles, cast on 86 sts.

Work in Twisted 2 x 2 rib as follows:

Row 1: *K2 tbl, P2*, repeat from * to * to end.

Repeat Row 1 17 times more, inc 1 st at centre of last row (87 sts).

Change to 6 mm (UK 4, US 10) knitting needles and work in st st for 2 rows.

Now work from Chart 1, joining in Calot and using the stranding method when working fairisle patterns.

When Chart 1 is complete, break Adriatique and continue for 6 rows in Calot.

CHART 1

Now work from Chart 2 joining in Avalanche. Carry yarn not in use carefully up the side of the work.

CHART 2

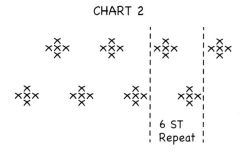

Cont working from Chart 2 until you have 7 rows of small snowflakes.

Work 5 rows st st in Calot.

Join in Adriatique and work from Chart 3.

CHART 3

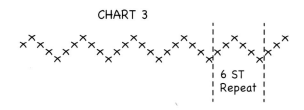

Continue in Calot for 7 rows st st.

Wind three small balls of Avalanche and use a separate ball for each of the large snowflakes.

Work from Chart 4 (over page) and place the snowflakes as follows:

Row 1: K5, work across 23 sts from chart, K4, work across 23 sts from chart, K4, work across 23 sts from chart, K5.

This now sets the placing of the charts. Continue working until all rows are complete.

CHART 4

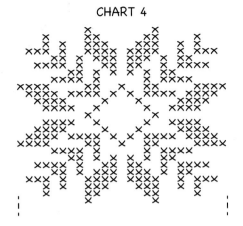

Work 3 rows in Calot. ****

Now work from Chart 2.

CHART 2

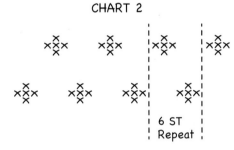

6 ST
Repeat

Shape Shoulders

Cast off 9 sts at beg of next 6 rows.

Leave remaining sts on a holder.

Front

Work as for back to ****

Shape Neck as follows:

Keeping continuity of the pattern correct, work across next 32 sts, put remaining sts onto a stitch holder and work this side first.

Dec 1 st at neck edge on the next 3 rows, the dec 1st at the same edge on next and every

following alt row until 27 sts remain, ending on a purl row.

Shape Shoulders

Cast off 9 sts at beg of next 3 rows. Fasten off.

Slip next 23 sts onto holder for centre of neck, rejoin yarn to last set of stitches and work to end of row. Now complete to match first side.

SLEEVES

Make 2

Using Adriatic and 5.5 mm (UK 5, US 9) knitting needles, cast on 40 sts.

Work in K2, P2 twisted rib for 14 rows as follows:

Row 1: K2tbl, P2.

Repeat Row 1 13 times more, and increase 1 st in centre of last row (41 sts).

Change to 6 mm (UK 4, US 10) knitting needles and work 2 rows in st st.

Join in Calot and work from chart 5.

Use the stranding method when working the fairisle pattern. Continue from the chart, adding increased stitches into the pattern as you work, and inc 1 st at each end on every 4th row to 67 sts.

Cont working in patt until work measures 54 cm (21 in) or desired length ending on a purl row. Adjust length here, if desired. Cast off.

Join other shoulder seam. Working from the inside of the sweater, fold the neckband in half onto the WS, now catch down each stitch, matching it stitch for stitch from the top and bottom. Don't pull the yarn too tightly, you need to retain enough stretch in the neckband to allow it to pull easily over the head. Join seam of neckband.

Work in all ends. Fold sleeve in half and mark centre point of top. With RS together, pin sleeve in place on back and front of sweater, making sure that it is equal on both sides. Stitch carefully in place. Do the same with the other sleeve on the opposite side of the sweater. Now join the side and sleeve seams. Press lightly under a damp cloth with a warm iron to flatten out the patterning.

NECKBAND AND MAKING UP

Join left shoulder seam.

Using Adriatique and 5.5 mm (UK 5, US 9) knitting needles, and with RS facing, pick up and knit 17 sts down left side of neck, 23 sts from holder on front neck, 17 sts up right front, and 32 sts from back neck.

Now proceed in K2tbl, P2 rib for 20 rows. Do not cast off. Run a contrast yarn through the stitches on the needle and slip them off.

Beanies for Men and Women

Designed to keep your head warm on cooler days, this pattern gives you a set of instructions to make a hat for both a man and a woman. A neat four-row pattern is worked to give a textured and extra warm turn-back cuff. Simple stitches are used so that a novice knitter will be able to make them. The range of colours in this yarn are stunning and you can chose either plain or tweed shades, so there is sure to be something to suit all tastes.

MATERIALS

- 1 x 100 g (3 1/2 oz) ball Stylecraft Alpaca DK, shade 6022, Red**

- Knitting needles: Size 3.75 mm (UK 9, US 5)

** Any DK weight yarn may be substituted for this design as long as you work to the tension stated.

TENSION

24 sts x 30 rows measures 10 cm (4 in) when knitted using 3.75 mm (UK 9, US 5) knitting needles.

MEASUREMENTS

To fit an average adult's head.

ABBREVIATIONS

See Knitting Terminology (page 24).

Pattern for cuff of hat

Row 1: Knit

Row 2: Knit

Row 3: P2, *K2, P2; rep from * to end.

Row 4: K2, *P2, K2; rep from * to end.

Man's Hat

Cast on 128 sts using recommended needle size and colour of your choice.

Work in 4-row patt for cuff until piece measures 14 cm (5½ in) ending on Row 2 of pattern.

Change to st st and work straight until piece measures 22 cm (9 in) ending on a purl row.

Shape Crown as follows:

Next row: (K10, K2tog, K11, K2tog) 5 times. Knit to end.

Next row and every following alternate row: Purl.

Next row: (K9, K2tog, K10, K2tog) 5 times, knit to end.

Cont decreasing in this way on every alternate row until 17 sts remain.

Break off yarn and thread through stitches left, pull up tight and fasten off.

Woman's Hat

Using 3.75mm needles cast on 116 sts, with recommended knitting needles and colour of your choice.

Work in cuff pattern for 12 cm (5 in) ending on Row 2 of pattern.

Change to st st

Work straight until piece measures 20 cm (8 in).

Shape Crown as follows:

Next row: K9, K2tog, (K9, K2tog, K10, K2tog) 4 times, K9, K2tog, knit to end.

Next and all following alternate rows: Purl.

Next row: K8, K2tog, (K8, K2tog, K9, K2tog) 4 times, K8, K2tog, knit to end.

Cont to dec sts in this way on every alternate row until 16 sts remain.

Break yarn and run through remaining sts, draw up tightly and secure.

TO MAKE UP

Work in any ends neatly. Join seam of hat, reversing the seam for the turn back on the cuff. Turn back cuff onto right side of hat.

Stripy Mittens

These fun stripy mittens will keep your hands warm on the coldest of winter days. Worked in plain stocking stitch with a neat twisted rib on the cuffs, you can make them in just a couple of evenings. The yarn is soft pure wool, which comes in an array of gorgeous colours. You can, of course, use just one shade of yarn, if you prefer.

Skill Level: Intermediate××

MATERIALS

- 1 x 50 g (2 oz) ball Wendy Merino DK (8-ply)*, shade 2378, Funghi

- 1 x 50 g (2 oz) ball Wendy Merino DK (8-ply)*, shade 2365, Birch

- 1 x 50 g (2 oz) ball Wendy Merino DK (8-ply)*, shade 2383, Watermelon

- Knitting needles: Sizes 3.75 mm (UK 9, US 5) and 4 mm (UK 8, US 6)

* You may substitute any DK (8-ply) weight yarn for these mittens as long as you work to a similar tension.

TENSION

22 sts x 30 rows measures 10 cm (4 in) using 4 mm knitting needles.

MEASUREMENTS

To fit: woman's average hand.

69

ABBREVIATIONS

See Knitting Terminology (page 24).

SPECIAL ABBREVIATIONS

Tw2: Worked over the next 2 sts as follows: Knit into front of second st, do not slip st off the needle, knit into first stitch in the usual way. Slip both sts off the needle at the same time.

M1: Increase 1 st by picking up the strand that lies between the stitch you are working and the next stitch then knitting into the back of it.

Right Hand

Using 3.75 mm (UK 9, US 5) and Funghi, cast on 40 sts.

Rows 1–2: *K2, P2*, rep from * to * to end.

Row 3: *Tw2, P2*, rep from * to * to end.

Row 4: *K2, P2* rep from * to * to end.

Repeat Rows 3–4 for pattern.

Work another 18 rows and increase 6 sts evenly across last row of rib (46 sts).

Change to 4 mm (UK 8, US 6) knitting needles and st st.

NOTE: Work in a pattern sequence of 4 rows watermelon, 4 rows birch, 4 rows funghi throughout,

Work 8 rows st st. **

Shape Thumb

Row 1: K23, m1, K3, m1, knit to end.

Work 3 rows st st.

Row 5: K23, m1, K5, m1, knit to end.

Row 6 and following alternate rows: Purl.

Row 7: K23, m1, K7, m1, knit to end.

Cont to inc 2 sts as set in every following alternate row until you have 56 sts ending on a purl row.

Work 2 rows st st.

Divide for Thumb

Next row: K38, turn.

*** Next row: P15, turn. Working on these 15 sts only, work 14 rows without shaping. (you will now work thumb in Funghi only and not stripes)

Next row: K1, *K2tog, repeat from * to end of row, break yarn, run through sts, draw up and secure.

With RS facing, rejoin yarn at base of thumb. Continue across stitches (43 sts).

Continue on these sts until a total of 11 stripes have been worked.

Shape Top

Row 1: K1, skpso, K16, K2tog, K1, skpso, K16, K2tog, K1.

Row 2 and following alternate rows: Purl.

Row 3: K1, skpso, K14, K2tog, K1, skpso, K14, K2tog, K1.

Row 5: K1, skpso, K12, K2tog, K1, skpso, K12, K2tog, K1.

Row 7: K1, skpso, K10, K2tog, K1, skpso K10, K2tog, K1.

Row 8: Purl (27 sts). Cast off.

Left Hand

Work as given for Right-hand Mitten to **

Shape Thumb

Row 1: K20, m1, K3, m1, knit to end.

Work 3 rows st st.

Row 5: K20, m1, K5, m1, knit to end.

Row 6 and following alternate rows: Purl.

Row 7: K20, m1, K7, m1, knit to end.

Cont to increase 2 sts as set in every following alternate row until there are 56 sts.

Work 2 rows st st.

Divide for Thumb

Next row: K35, turn.

Now complete from *** as given for Right-hand Mitten.

TO MAKE UP

Turn mitten with RS tog. Sew seams neatly. Turn RS out. Press lightly under a damp cloth with a warm iron. Repeat with other mitten.

Alpaca Scarf

Pure soft alpaca yarn is used to make this attractive masculine scarf. The broken rib pattern is made up of four-row repeats so a novice knitter can attempt the design. I chose grey but there are more lovely shades in the range of yarn so you are sure to find one to suit your tastes.

MATERIALS

- 4 x 50 g (2 oz) balls King Cole Baby Alpaca, shade 502, Grey*

- Knitting needles: size 4.5 mm (UK 7, US 7)

*Alpaca is a luxurious yarn and the dense fibres produce an incredibly soft and warm finish to the garment. You must take care when washing and drying items made with this yarn. Substitute any DK (8-ply) weight yarn, if desired.

TENSION

22 sts and 30 rows to 10 cm (4 in) measured over pattern when slightly stretched using 4.5 mm (UK 7, US 7) knitting needles.

MEASUREMENTS

Finished length: approximately 1.5 m (5 ft).

ABBREVIATIONS

See Knitting Terminology (page 24).

Scarf

Using 4.5 mm (UK 7, US 7) knitting needles, cast on 54 sts.

Row 1: Knit.

Row 2: Knit.

Row 3: P2, *K2, P2; rep from * to end.

Row 4: K2, *P2, K2; rep from * to end.

These 4 rows form the pattern and are repeated throughout.

Continue in pattern until work measures 1.5 m (60 in), or required length.

Work 2 rows garter st. Cast off.

TO MAKE UP AND FRINGE

Work in ends neatly on scarf. To make a fringe, wind yarn around a book or piece of cardboard six times and knot through row ends of the scarf on the garter st rows. Add approximately 14 fringes to each end.

Hot Water Bottle Cover

Two complementary shades and a neat slipped-stitch pattern are used to create this cuddly hot water bottle cover. It's just the thing to warm your toes as well as your heart on cold winter nights. Although the pattern looks complicated it is, in fact, a simple four-row pattern repeat and can be attempted by a knitter with a little experience. Pom-pom ties complete the look.

MATERIALS

- 2 x 50 g (2 oz) balls Bergere de France Magic+ Chunky, shade 29040, Calot (A)*

- 2 x 50 g (2 oz) balls Bergere de France Magic+ Chunky, shade 20739, Avalanche (B)*

- Knitting needles: size 5.5 mm (UK 5, US 9)

- Knitting needles: size 5 mm (UK 6, US 8)

*You may substitute any chunky-weight yarn for this design as long as you work to a similar tension.

TENSION

16 sts x 22 rows measures 10 cm (4 in) when knitted using 5.5 mm (UK 5, US 9) knitting needles.

MEASUREMENTS

To fit: Average hot water bottle.

ABBREVIATIONS

See Knitting Terminology (page 24).

Cover

Make 2 pieces alike.

Using 5.5 mm (UK 5, US 9) knitting needles and yarn B, cast on 39 sts.

Work 4 rows in garter st.

Change to patt as follows:

Row 1 (WS): Using yarn A, P1, yb, sl 1, yf, *P3, yb, sl 1, yf , rep from * to last st, p1.

Row 2: K1, sl1, *K3, sl 1, rep from * to last st, K1.

Row 3: Change to yarn B and P3, * yb, sl 1, yf, P3, rep from * to end.

Row 4: K3, *sl1, K3, rep from * to end.

These 4 rows form the pattern and are repeated.

Continue in patt until work measures 25 cm (10 in).

Keeping patt correct, dec 1 st at each end of next row, and following 2 alt rows.

Change to 5 mm (UK 6, US 8) knitting needles, and using yarn B only, work in K2, P2 rib, dec 1 st in the centre of the first row.

Cont for another 25 rows. Break off yarn B.

Join in yarn A and work 4 rows K2, P2 rib. Cast off.

TO MAKE UP

Sew in ends. Now place back and front pieces RS tog and edges aligned and sew side seams and base. Note that the seam on the ribbed top will need to be reversed for turn over. Make a twisted chain using Calot yarn. Using a large-eyed blunt-ended needle, thread the chain through the ribbing at the top of the cover. Attach a small pom pom to each end of the chain. Fold the ribbed top over onto the RS of the cover. The top is stretchy enough to pull the cover on to the hot water bottle. Tie the chain in a bow.

Pocket Scarf

Not only will this super warm scarf keep your neck warm but it also has deep pockets to keep your hands warm as well. Add a choice of pocket to the scarf to make the look masculine or feminine. A gorgeous soft pure wool in a chunky weight means this scarf is sure to keep you warm on even the coldest days.

MATERIALS

- 7 x 50 g (2 oz) balls of Drops Eskimo chunky yarn*:

- For the man's version, shade 82, Winter Fog

- For the woman's version, shade 35, Lime

- Knitting needles: size 5.5 mm (UK 5, US 9) and size 5 mm (UK 6, US 8)

- Cable needle

* You can substitute any chunky-weight yarn as long as you check the tension.

MEASUREMENTS

170 x 20 cm (64 x 8 in)

SPECIAL ABBREVIATIONS

C8B: Cable 8 sts back as follows: slip next 4 sts onto cable needle and leave at back of work, knit next 4 sts, then knit 4 sts from cable needle.

C8F: Cable 8 front as follows: Slip next 4 sts onto cable needle and leave at front of work, knit next 4 sts, then knit 4 sts from cable needle.

Tw2f: Twist 2 front worked over next 2 sts as follows: knit into front of second st, do not slip off needles, knit first st as usual, then slip both sts of needle together.

Tw2b: Twist 2 back worked over next 2 sts as follows: knit into the back of the second st, now knit into front of first st in the usual way. Slip both sts off the needle together.

MB: Make bobble as follows: K1, P1, K1, all into next st, turn and K3, turn and P3, slip second and third sts over first st.

Basic Scarf

Using size 5.5 mm (UK 6, US 9) knitting needles and yarn, cast on 28 sts.

Work 6 rows garter st.

Row 1: Knit.

Row 2: K5, P18, K5.

Repeat these 2 rows 17 times more.

Now work 8 rows garter st.

*** Work Rows 1 and 2 nine times.

Now work 8 rows garter st. ***

Repeat from *** to *** eight times more.

Next row: Knit.

Next row: K5, P18, K5.

Repeat these 2 rows 17 times more.

Work 6 rows garter st. Cast off.

Pockets

WOMAN'S POCKET

Make 2

Pattern Panel for Flower Motif is worked over 15 sts.

Row 1 (RS): P6, K1, P1, K1, P6.

Row 2: K5, P2, K1, P2, K5.

Row 3: P4, K2tog, K1, yrn, P1, yfwd, K1, K2togtbl, P4. This is correct now.

Row 4: K4, P3, K1, P3, K4.

Row 5: P3, K2tog, K1, yfwd, K1, P1, K1, yfwd, K1, K2togtbl, P3.

Row 6: K3, P4, K1, P4, K3.

Row 7: P2, K2tog, K1, yfwd, K2, P1, K2, yfwd, K1, K2togtbl, P2.

Row 8: K2, P5, K1, P5, K2.

Row 9: P1, K2tog, K1, yfwd, K3, P1, K3, yfwd, K1, K2togtbl, P1.

Row 10: K1, P6, K1, P6, K1.

Row 11: K2tog, K1, yfwd, K4, P1, K4, yfwd, K1, K2togtbl.

Row 12: P7, K1, P7.

Row 13: K4, K2tog, K1, yfwd, K1, yfwd, K1, K2togtbl, K4.

Row 14: P6, K1, P1, K1, P6.

Row 15: K3, K2tog, K1, yrn, P1, K1, P1, yfwd, K1, K2togtbl, K3.

Row 16: P5, K2, P1, K2, P5.

Row 17: K2, K2tog, K1, yrn, P2, K1, P2, yfwd, K1, K2togtbl, K2.

Row 18: P4, K3, P1, K3, P4.

Row 19: K1, K2tog, K1, yrn, P2, MB, K1, MB, P2, yfwd, K1, K2togtbl, K1.

Row 20: P3, K3, P1, K1, P1, K3, P3.

Row 21: K2tog, K1, yrn, P1, MB, P5, MB, P1, yfwd, K1, K2togtbl.

Row 22: P1, K13, P1.

Row 23: P3, MB, P7, MB.

Row 24: K15.

Row 25: As Row 23.

Row 26: as Row 24.

Row 27: P4, MB, P5, MB, P4.

Row 28: As Row 24.

Row 29: P6, MB, P1, MB, P6

Using 5.5 mm (UK 6, US 9) knitting needles and yarn, cast on 29 sts.

Work 6 rows garter st.

Next row (RS): K5, P19, K5.

Next row: Knit.

Repeat the last 2 rows once more.

Begin pattern panel and at the same time keep 5 sts in garter st and 2 sts in reversed st st on each side of the panel as you work. I suggest you place a marker on each side of these 7 sts to enable you to follow the pattern panel more easily.

Row 1: K5, P2, slip marker. Work Row 1 of pattern panel, slip marker, P2, K5.

Row 2: K7, slip marker, work Row 2 of pattern panel, slip marker, K7.

Cont as set until the 29th row of the pattern panel has been completed.

Next row: Knit.

Next row: K5, P19, K5.

Now work 6 rows garter st. Cast off.

MAN'S POCKET

Make 2

Using 5.5 mm (UK 6, US 9) knitting needles and yarn, cast on 28 sts.

Work 6 rows garter st.

Inc Row: K5, P2, inc in each of next 4 sts, P2, inc in each of next 2 sts, P2, inc in each of next 4 sts, P2, K5.

Begin cable pattern panel as follows:

Row 1 (WS): K7, P8, K2, P4, K2, P8, K7.

Row 2: K5, P2, C8B, P2, tw2f, tw2b, P2, C8F, P2, K5.

Row 3: K7, P8, K2, P4, K2, P8, K7.

Row 4: K5, P2, K8, P2, tw2b, tw2f, P2, K8, P2, K5.

Row 5: As Row 3.

Row 6: K5, P2, K8, P2, tw2f, tw2b, P2, K8, P2, K5.

Row 7: As Row 3.

Row 8: As Row 4.

Row 9: As Row 3.

Rows 2–9 form the patt repeat. Repeat them 3 more times then work Rows 2 and 3 once.

Next row: K5, P2, K2tog 4 times, P2, K2tog twice, P2, K2tog 4 times, P2, K5.

Next row: Knit.

Work 6 more rows of garter st. Cast off.

TO MAKE UP

Work in any ends neatly. Pin the pockets on each end of the scarf. Sew in place.

Snood

A blend of lambswool and kid mohair yarn are used to knit this gorgeously soft snood. I have chosen a dusky pink shade but there are plenty of beautiful colours to chose from in the yarn range. The lacy pattern is quite simple and you can add extra length to the finished project easily.

MATERIALS

- 3 x 50 g balls Rowan Kid Classic, shade 854, Tea Rose

- Knitting needles: size 5.5 mm (UK 5, US 9)

* You may substitute the yarn with and aran weight , just check tension before you begin.

TENSION

19 sts x 25 rows = 10 cm (4 in) using 5.5 mm (UK 5, US 9) knitting needles.

MEASUREMENTS

50 x 60 cm (20 x 24 in).

ABBREVIATIONS

See Knitting Terminology (page 24).

Snood

Using recommended knitting needles, cast on 72 sts.

Knit 4 rows.

Begin patt as follows:

Row 1: Knit.

Row 2: Purl.

Row 3: K2, *yrn, P1, P3tog, P1, yon, K2 * rep from * to * to end.

Row 4: Purl.

These 4 rows form the lacy pattern.

Repeat these 4 rows another 4 times.

Now work 4 rows in garter st.**

Repeat from ** to ** another 4 times, and then cast off.

Note: You can easily add extra length to the snood by adding extra pattern repeats, if you like.

TO MAKE UP

Sew in ends and then neatly sew the long side seam, matching patterns as you work.

Slouchy Beanie

A simple two-row pattern makes this project ideal for the novice knitter. Big needles and a deliciously soft chunky yarn mean that the hat will only take a couple of evenings to complete. I have chosen a lovely indigo blue shade for my hat.

MATERIALS

- 1 x 100 g (3 1/2 oz) ball Wendy Aspire Chunky, shade 3246, Indigo*

- Knitting needles: Sizes 5 mm (UK 6, US 8) and 6.5 mm (UK 3, US 10 ½)

* You can substitute any chunky weight yarn for this project as long as it knits to a similar tension.

TENSION

14 sts x 22 rows measure 10 cm (4 in) using 6.5 mm (UK 3, US 10½) knitting needles.

MEASUREMENTS

To fit average woman's head.

ABBREVIATIONS

See Knitting Terminology (page 24).

Beanie

Using 5 mm (UK 6, US 8) knitting needles, cast on 72 sts.

Work in K2, P2 rib for 7 rows.

Next row: *Rib 5, inc in next st, repeat to end (84 sts).

Change to 6.5 mm (UK 3, US 10½) knitting needles and proceed as follows:

Row 1: (RS) P3, K3.

Row 2: Knit.

Repeat these two rows until work measures 23 cm (9 in) ending on a Row 2 pattern.

Shape Top

Next row: *K2, K2tog, repeat from * to end (63 sts).

Work 5 rows in garter st.

Next row: K2, K2tog, to last 3 sts, K3 (48 sts).

Work 5 rows garter st.

Next row: K2, K2tog to end (36 sts).

Work 3 rows garter st.

Next row: K2, K2tog to end (27 sts).

Work 3 rows garter st.

Next row: K2tog across row to last st K1. Break yarn and run through sts on needle, draw up and fasten off.

TO MAKE UP

Work in any ends neatly. Sew side seam on beret.

Shoulder Wrap

This pretty shoulder wrap is just the thing to bring that extra bit of warmth on chilly days. A combination of stitch patterns are used to create it, but they are simple to work so the project can be attempted by the not-so-experienced knitter. Big needles and chunky yarn make this a quick knit. I have chosen a rich red colour but there are plenty more shades to choose from.

Skill Level: Intermediate ××

MATERIALS

- 3 x 100 g (3 1/2 oz) balls of Robin Chunky Yarn, shade 32*

* Any chunky yarn can be substituted for this project as long as you work to the stated tension in the pattern.

- Knitting needles: size 6.5 mm (UK 3, US 10½)

TENSION

14 st x 20 rows measures 10 cm (4 in) when knitted using 6.5 mm (UK 3, US 10½) knitting needles.

MEASUREMENTS

139 x 54 cm (56 x 21 in).

ABBREVIATIONS

See Knitting Terminology (page 24).

Shoulder Wrap

Using 6.5 mm (UK 3, US 10½) knitting needles, cast on 2 sts.

Proceed in Stitch Pattern moss stitch (US seed stitch)

Next row: Inc in first st, K1.

Next row: K1, P1, K1.

Next row: Inc in first st, P1, K1.

Next row: K1, P1, K1, P1.

Cont in moss stitch and at the same time increase 1 st at beg of every other row until there are 48 sts, working the extra stitches into the pattern as they are increased.

Change to Stitch Pattern 2 ,and at the same time, maintain the increased stitch at the same edge as before until there are 72 sts.

Stitch Pattern 2

Rows 1–4: K4, P4.

Rows 5–8: P4, K4.

These 8 rows form the pattern.

Keeping pattern correct , dec 1 st at beg of shaped edge on every other row, as before, until there are 48 sts.

Change to **Stitch Pattern 1**.

Keeping pattern correct, continue to decrease at the same edge as before until there are 2 sts left, work 2tog and fasten off.

Work in any ends neatly. Add a fringe to the wrap, if you like, by cutting equal lengths of yarn and knotting them through the shaped edge.

Poncho

Pure wool/alpaca mix chunky roving yarn is used for this attractive poncho. A deep patterned band knitted sideways forms the base of the garment and then the remaining part is picked up and knitted in the usual way. The poncho is completed with a cosy turn-over collar.

MATERIALS

- 7 x 100 g (3 1/2 oz) balls Wendy Aspire Chunky yarn, shade 3243.*

* Any chunky weight yarn can be substituted for this project as long as you work to a similar tension.

- Knitting needles: size 6.5 mm (UK 3/US 10½)

- Circular knitting needle: 6.5 mm (UK 3/US 10½)

TENSION

14 sts x 20 rows measures 10 cm/4 in square when knitted using 6.5 mm (UK 3/US 10½) knitting needles.

MEASUREMENTS

M/L woman

ABBREVIATIONS

See Knitting Terminology (page 24).

Poncho

Begin with Lower Band.

Using 6.5 mm (UK 3/US 10½), cast on 42 sts.

Row 1 (RS): K3, P5, yfwd, skpo, K5, K2tog, yrn, P8, yfwd, skpo, K5, K2tog, yrn, P5, K3.

Row 2 and all even rows: K8, P9, K8, P9, K8.

Row 3: K3, P5, K1, yfwd, skpo, K3, K2tog, yfwd, K1, P8, K1, yfwd, skpo, K3, K2tog, yfwd, K1, P5, K3.

Row 5: K3, P5, K2, yfwd, skpo, K1, K2tog, yfwd, K2, P8, K2, yfwd, skpo, K1, K2tog, yfwd, K2, P5, K3.

Row 7: K3, P5, K3, yfwd, sl 1, K2tog, psso , yfwd, K3, P8, K3, yfwd, sl 1, K2tog, psso, yfwd, K1, P5, K3.

Row 8: K8, P9, K8, P9, K8.

These 8 rows form the pattern and are repeated. Continue in pattern until work measures 127 cm (50 in) ending on a Row 8. Cast off.

Join band into a circle by sewing the short end of the piece. The seam will be at the centre back of the poncho.

Beginning at centre back seam, with right side facing and using circular needle, pick up and knit 176 sts from one long edge of the band (be careful not to twist work when beginning to knit.)

Continue in reverse st st (purl side is right side of work) until work measures 32 cm (13 in) from base ending on a wrong side row.

Shape Top

Next row: *P9, P2tog, rep from * to end.

Work 5 rows rev st st.

Next row: *P8, P2tog, rep from * to end

Work 5 rows rev st st.

Next row: *P7, P2tog, rep from * to end.

Work 5 rows rev st st.

Continue to decrease as set on every sixth row until there are 112 sts.

Change to K2, P2 rib and work for 25 cm (10 in). Cast off. Work in ends neatly. Fold over the garter stitch border at the base of the poncho onto the wrong side of the work and slip stitch in place to form hem.

Boot Toppers

Keep your legs extra warm this winter with these gorgeous textured boot toppers. Made in a lovely aran-weight alpaca mix yarn they knit up quite quickly. The pattern is a little complicated but well worth the time taken when you see the finished project. The colours in the yarn range are lovely misty shades.

MATERIALS

- 1 x 100 g (3 1/2 oz) ball Rowan Creative Worsted, shade 0712, Lavender Heather

* You can substitute any aran-weight yarn for this project as long as you work to a similar tension. Tension is not critical on this project.

- Knitting needles: size 5 mm (UK 6, US 8)

- 2 stitch markers

- Buttons (optional)

TENSION

20 sts x 24 rows measure 10 cm (4 in) when knitted using size 5 mm (UK 6, US 8) knitting needles.

MEASUREMENTS

S / M / L to fit leg calf circumference 34 /36/ 38 cm (13½ /14 /14½ in). Depth: 20 cm (8 in).

ABBREVIATIONS

See Knitting Terminology (page 24).

SPECIAL ABBREVIATIONS

W4: Wrap 4: Insert right-hand needle between 4th and 5th sts on left-hand needle and K1, drawing up a longer st than normal. K4, sl 1 loop of long stitch over the 4 sts to wrap them.

Boot Toppers

Make 2

Using 5 mm (UK 6, US 8) knitting needles, cast on 35 sts.

Knit 1 row.

When following pattern, work the 5 sts at each end of the row in garter stitch. Move markers at the appropriate place on every row.

Row 1: K5 (place marker) *K4, P2*, repeat from * to * to last 6 sts, K1, (place marker), K5.

Rows 2 and 4: (K5 for border), P1, *K2, P4*, repeat from * to * to last 5 sts, (K5 for border).

Row 3: (K5 for border) *W4, P2*, repeat from * to * ending K1, (K5 for border).

Rows 5 and 11: K5 for border. Knit to last 5 sts, (K5 for border).

Rows 6 and 12: (K5 for border), purl to last 5 sts, (K5 for border).

Row 7: (K5 for border), K1, *P2, K4*, repeat from * to * to last 5 sts, (K5 for border).

Rows 8 and 10: (K5 for border), *P4, K2*, repeat from * to * to last 6 sts, K1, (K5 for border).

Row 9: (K5 for border) K1, *P2, work wrap 4 as before*, rep from * to * to last 5 sts, (K5 for border).

These 12 rows form pattern and border pattern. Continue as set for another 34, 35, 37 cm (13½, 14, 14½ in), ending on a Row 6 or 12.

Knit 1 row and cast off.

TO MAKE UP

Join short side of work neatly.

Angora Ankle Socks

Sumptuous Angora yarn is used to knit these cosy ankle socks. The silky softness will be sure to keep toes warm during the coldest weather. A simple ridged panel brings added interest to the design and a turn over cuff at the top will keep ankles snug.

Skill Level: Intermediate ××

MATERIALS

- Yarn: Any DK weight can be substituted for the yarn used although you will not get the gorgeous softness produced by angora. As a side note I would like to say that the angora yarn I have used comes from a source where the animals that produce the yarn are treated with the greatest respect and care.

- 1 x 50grm ball of St Magnus 50/50 Angora yarn shade Eau de nil

- Needles size 4.00 (UK 8, US 6)

- Needles size 3.75m (UK 9, US 5)

TENSION

24st x 30 rows measure 10cm (4in) using 4.00m (UK 8, US 6) needles.

MEASUREMENTS

To fit average ladies foot.

ABBREVIATIONS

See Knitting Terminology (page 24).

Sock Instructions (Make 2 alike)

With 3.75m (UK 9, US 5) needles cast on 52 sts fairly loosely.

Work in K2, P2 rib for 10 cms (4 in)

Change to 4.0m (UK 8, US 6) needles

Next Row: K13, P2, K22, P2, K13

Next Row: P13, K2, P22, K2, P13.

Begin Pattern as follows:

Row 1: K13, P24, K13.

Row 2: P13.K2, P22, K2, P13.

Row 3: K13, P2, K22, P2, K13

Row 4: P13.K2, P22, K2, P13.

These 4 rows form the ridge pattern and are repeated.

Continue in pattern until work measures 15cm (6in)

Divide for heel

Knit 13 (for first half of heel) slip next 26 sts onto a stitch holder (for instep) slip rem 13 sts onto a second stitch holder (for second half of heel)

First half of heel

Return to first set of 13sts on needle, and

proceed as follows.

Row 1: (WS) Sl 1 p12.

Row 2: Knit.

Repeat these 2 rows 6 times more, then work row 1 once more.

Turn heel

Row 1: (RS) k2, skpso, k1, turn,

Row 2: Sl1, P3, turn,

Row 3: K3, skpso, K1, Turn

Row 4: Sl1, P4, turn.

Row 5: k4, skpso, K1, turn.

Row 6: Sl 1, P5,

Row 7: K5, skpso, K1, Turn

Row 8: Sl1, P6, turn,

Row 9: K6, skpso

Row 10: Sl 1, P7.

Break yarn and place remaining 8 sts onto a holder.

Second half of heel

With RS facing place 13 sts held for second half of heel on larger needle, join in yarn and knit to end.

Row 1: Purl.

Row 2: Sl 1. K 12.

Rep these 2 rows 7 more times,

Turn Heel.

Row 1: (WS) P2, P2tog, P1. Turn,

Row 2: Sl 1. K3, turn,

Row 3: P3, p2tog. P1. Turn.

Row 4: Sl 1, K4, Turn,

Row 5: P4, p2tog, p1, turn.

Row 6: Sl 1. K5, turn,

Row 7: P5, p2tog, p1, turn,

Row 8: Sl 1, K6, turn.

Row 9: P8

Break yarn and place rem sts on to holder.

GUSSET

With RS facing, rejoin yarn and K 8sts of first half of heel from holder, pick and k6 sts along edge of first half of heel, pattern across 26 sts of instep from holder, pick up and knit 6 sts along edge of second half of heel, k 8sts of second half of heel from holder. (54 sts.)

*NOTE * Keep continuity of the ridge pattern over the centre 26 sts

Next row and following alternate rows. Purl.

Row 3: (RS). K 12, K2tog, pattern 26, skpso, K 12.

Row 5: K 11. K2tog, pattern 26, skpso, K11.

Row 7: K10, K2tog, pattern 26, skpso, K 10

Row 9: K9. K2tog, pattern 26, skpso K9,

Row 11: K8, K2tog, pattern 26, skpso K8. 44sts

Row 12: Purl, Heel shaping is now complete.

Continue on these sts, keeping continuity of ridge pattern over the centre 26 sts.

Work a further 24 rows.

SHAPE TOE.

Row 1: K8, K2tog, K2, skpo, K17, K2tog, pm, k2, pm, skpo, K8. (40 sts.)

Row 2: and all alternate WS side rows Purl.

Row 3: * Knit to 2sts before marker, K2tog, slip marker, knit to next marker, skpso; rep from * once, knit to end. (36 sts.)

Repeat last 2 rows 4 times more, then work row 2 once more, (20 sts.) Cast off.

TO MAKE UP

Sew in ends neatly. Using a flat seam join toe seam, now join the foot and leg seam in the same way. Turn over cuff at ankle.

Hot Water Bottle Cover

Autumnal shades and a chunky cable pattern make this hot water bottle cover a pleasure to cuddle up with. The yarns used are beautifully soft and contain alpaca but you can always substitute these with an aran-weight yarn that has a similar tension, if you like.

MATERIALS

- 1 x 50 g (2 oz) ball Rowan Felted Tweed Aran, shade 720, Pebble (A)

- 2 x 50 g (2 oz) balls Rowan Felted Tweed Aran, shade 721, Cork (C)

- 1 x 50 g (2 oz) ball Rowan Kid Classic Aran, shade 872, Earth (B)

* You may substitute any similar weight yarn as long as your tension matches that stated in the pattern.

- Knitting needles: size 5 mm (UK 6, US 8) and size 4 mm (UK 8, US 6)

- Cable needle

TENSION

16 sts x 23 rows measure 10 cm (4 in) when knitted using size 4 mm (UK 8, US 6) knitting needles.

MEASUREMENTS

To fit an average hot water bottle.

SPECIAL ABBREVIATIONS

C4F: Slip next 2 sts onto a cable needle and leave at front of work, knit next 2 sts, then knit 2 sts from cable needle.

C4B: Slip next 2 sts onto a cable needle and leave at back of work, knit next 2 sts, then knit 2 sts from cable needle.

Moss stitch: Row 1 : * K1,P1, repeat from * to end. Row 1 is repeated for pattern.

Cover

Make 2 pieces alike.

Using 5 mm (UK 6, US 8) knitting needles and yarn C, cast on 35 sts.

Work 6 rows in moss stitch. Dec 1 st at centre of last row (34 sts).

Now begin cable pattern:

Row 1 (WS): Purl.

Row 2: P3, K4, *P4, K4*, repeat from * to * to last 3 sts, P3.

Repeat the last 2 rows twice more then Row 1 again.

Row 8: K3, P4, *K4, P4*, repeat from * to * to last 3 sts, K3.

Row 9: Purl.

Row 10: K1, *C4F, C4B*, repeat from * to * to last st, K1.

These 10 rows form the pattern. Repeat them once more. Break yarn C and join in yarn A.

Work 20 rows in pattern. Break yarn A and join in yarn B.

Work 20 rows in pattern

Next row: Purl using yarn B.

Change to 4 mm (UK 8, US 6) knitting needles and work ribbed top:

Break off yarn B and join in yarn C. Work in K2, P2 rib for 36 rows.

Cast off in rib.

Work other side to match.

Make bobbles:

Using yarn A and 4 mm (UK 8, US 6) knitting needles, cast on 4 sts.

Purl 1 row.

Next row: Knit twice into each st to end.

Next row: Purl.

Next row: Knit twice into each st to end.

Next row: Purl. Break yarn and run thread through sts on knitting needle, draw up tight to form a ball, stitch the side seam together.

TO MAKE UP

With RS facing inside sew pieces together matching stripes as you do. Turn right sides out and then turn over cuff at the top of the knitting. Make a tie by either working a crochet chain or make a twisted cord. Thread the tie through the top ribbing at regular intervals, using a large eyed blunt-ended needle. Attach a bobble to each end of the ties. Fasten with a bow.